FOOTBALL

The ultimate guide to the beautiful game

CLIVE GIFFORD

KINGFISHER

Foreword

Football is a wonderful game, a sport which knows
no boundaries of race, age, wealth, sex or religion.
Football is a sport which reaches everyone. All over
the world, people young and old, play it, watch
it and read about it. This book captures the
international appeal, enjoyment and excitement
of this unique sport.

People often forget that for all its drama and
beauty, football is a simple game built on a set of
individual skills, allied to working together as a team.
Although natural ability is a gift, players are not born
with these skills and understanding – they are
things which must be learned. To be a success
requires much hard work, patience, self-sacrifice and
a desire to study the game and improve. Most
importantly, it involves loving what you do. Young
people will continue to play and watch football, and
this book will help to increase their enjoyment of the
world's most beautiful game.

KINGFISHER

Kingfisher Publications Plc
New Penderel House
283-288 High Holborn
London WC1V 7HZ

www.kingfisherpub.com

Author Clive Gifford
Consultant Anthony Hobbs
Editors Clive Wilson, Matt Parselle
Design Mike Buckley, Malcolm Parchment
Production Controller Joanne Blackmore
DTP Manager Nicky Studdart
Picture Research Jane Lambert, Juliet Duff
Indexer Chris Bernstein

First published by Kingfisher Publications Plc 2002

10 9 8 7 6 5 4 3 2
2TR/1103/PROSP/CLSN*UD(CLSN)/157MA

Copyright © Kingfisher Publications Plc 2002
This updated edition published in 2004

A CIP catalogue record for this book is available from the British Library

ISBN 0 7534 0940 2
Printed in China

Contents

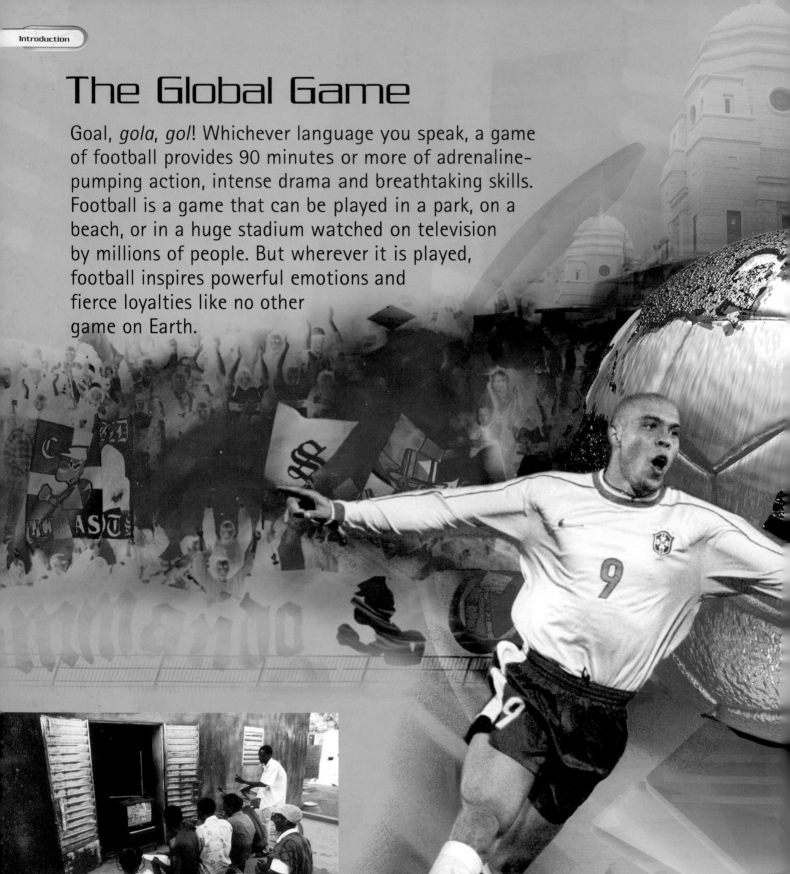

The Global Game

Goal, *gola*, *gol*! Whichever language you speak, a game of football provides 90 minutes or more of adrenaline-pumping action, intense drama and breathtaking skills. Football is a game that can be played in a park, on a beach, or in a huge stadium watched on television by millions of people. But wherever it is played, football inspires powerful emotions and fierce loyalties like no other game on Earth.

▲ Football crosses all boundaries. It is passionately followed by men, women, boys and girls of all ages and backgrounds. Television allows even the remotest places to have access to games from around the world.

▲ Ronaldo grew up in a poor district of Rio de Janeiro, Brazil. He secured a place in Brazil's 1994 World Cup squad at the age of 18. Since then, Ronaldo has played for clubs in Europe and has become one of the world's most feared strikers. He was leading scorer in the 2002 World Cup with eight goals.

Less is more

Football is essentially a simple game. The aim is to get the ball into the opponent's net, without using hands or arms. Whichever team scores the most goals wins! Of course, there are many rules and regulations, but these are designed to keep the game fair and flowing. Whatever your skill level, you can enjoy the game without expensive kit or equipment. You don't even need a proper pitch. All you need for a friendly game is a safe, open space or indoor sports hall, along with a ball, a few players and something to mark out a goal.

▲ Pelé described football as 'the beautiful game'. The outstanding Brazilian player from the late 1950s to the early 1970s, he is widely recognized as the greatest footballer in the history of the game.

"Some people think football is a matter of life and death. I don't like that attitude. I can assure them it is much more serious than that." Bill Shankly

"Football is like a religion to me. I worship the ball, and I treat it like a god." Pelé

▶ French fans celebrate their team's 3-0 victory over Brazil in the 1998 World Cup final. The match was watched by more than 600 million people around the world. In total, almost 1.5 billion viewers watched games in the 2002 World Cup held in Japan and South Korea.

Big business

Big clubs such as Spain's Real Madrid, England's Manchester United and Italy's AC Milan and Juventus are supported around the world. These clubs are run as powerful businesses that generate millions of pounds a year. Their top players are often as famous – and as well paid – as movie stars.

All over the world

From its official beginnings in Britain and mainland Europe in the 19th century, football has spread to almost every part of the world. Historically, South America and Europe have been football's powerhouses. However, the rise of women's football in the United States, and the emergence of great players and teams from nations in Africa, Asia, Australasia and the Middle East, have turned the game into a truly global sport.

From Earliest Beginnings

Football has ancient origins. More than 2,000 years ago, Chinese, Japanese, Greek and Roman cultures all featured games that involved players kicking or handling a ball through a goal. Later, in the Middle Ages, violent contests between two teams of unlimited numbers were often played in the streets of towns and villages. A pig's bladder or stuffed animal skin served as the ball. In the 1800s, football became organized with official rules. By the end of the century, it had evolved into more or less the game we play today.

▲ *A pig's bladder is blown up for a game of pallo. This 17th-century game, played in Europe, was an early version of football.*

The Football Association

In 1863, representatives of 11 English footballing sides met at the Freemason's Tavern in London to form the Football Association (FA). Until then, the hundreds of schools and clubs that played football each had their own set of rules. Some clubs played by rules that allowed handling the ball or tripping, for example, while others did not. Out of this chaos, the FA devised a single set of rules. Within a decade, the English FA was joined by FAs from Wales, Scotland and Ireland. In 1882, these four created the International Football Association Board (IFAB), which attempted to rule and regulate football across the world.

▲ *During the Victorian era, the typical outfit for football teams, such as the Scottish international side of 1892, included caps and knee breeches (long shorts).*

▲ *Dating from the 16th century, the annual Shrove Tuesday football game in the Derbyshire town of Ashbourne, England, has no referees and very few rules. The goals are placed at either end of the town and the teams are known as Up'ards and Down'ards.*

◄ *The Japanese game of kemari was developed from ball games played in Ancient China more than 2,000 years ago. In kemari, players had to pass the ball to each other without it touching the ground.*

Explosion in interest

Towards the end of the 19th century, football spread like wildfire around the globe, carried first by British traders and sailors, and then travellers from other European nations. The decades either side of 1900 saw dozens of countries, from Austria to Brazil, Hungary to Russia, form their own football teams, competitions and associations. In 1904, tired of the IFAB burying its head in the sand, the *Fédération Internationale de Football Association* (FIFA) was formed by France and six other European nations. Football was now a truly international sport.

◀▲ *Despite some opposition from the male-dominated establishment, women's football matches grew in popularity from the 1880s onwards.*

▶ *Until the 1940s, balls and boots were made from heavy, unwaterproof leather. On a wet pitch, both ball and boots would get much heavier and lose their shape.*

▲ *Shinpads were invented in 1874 by Samuel W. Widdowson, a Nottingham Forest forward who played for England in 1880.*

Early games and rules

Football matches from the 1870s and 1880s onwards attracted large crowds and much interest. Many of the basic rules of the game were in place by then. Modifications to the game such as two-handed throw-ins and penalty kicks were introduced. For a long time, goalkeepers could be charged and knocked over at any time; later, this was allowed only when they had the ball. However, goalkeepers could handle the ball anywhere on the pitch. This rule changed after a flood of goals were scored in 1910 by goalkeepers throwing the ball into the opposition's net!

▶ *The England shirt (right) was worn in the first official international match which was against Scotland in 1872. Before this date, caps were used to distinguish between teams. Caps then became rewards for playing for your country.*

Timeline

1848
First set of football rules drawn up at Cambridge University, England

1863
The Football Association formed in England

1871
Football's oldest surviving competition, the FA Cup, is created

1872
First football international – England 0 Scotland 0

1872
Corner kicks introduced for the first time

1878
Whistles first used by referees

1885
Paying players (professionalism) legalized

1891
Penalty kicks introduced

1899
FA suggest an upper limit of £10 on player transfer fees

1905
First South American international match – Uruguay v Argentina

1908
Football's first Olympic Games won by England

1910
The first Copa America won by Argentina

1912
Goalkeepers now allowed to handle the ball only in their own penalty area

1913
Ten-yards rule introduced for free kicks

1926
Legendary Brazilian footballer, Artur Friedenreich, hits 1,000th goal in Brazilian football

1930
First World Cup finals in Uruguay

See also

12-13 Key Rules

64-65 Tactics

Pitch and Players

The pitch – this is where it all happens, where players pit their skills against each other and where games are won and lost. For the professional game, you need two 11-a-side teams on a pitch about 100m long and 65–70m wide. These teams contest two halves of 45 minutes, plus injury or stoppage time.

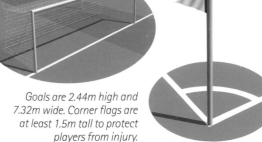

Goals are 2.44m high and 7.32m wide. Corner flags are at least 1.5m tall to protect players from injury.

The penalty spot is a circle marked out 10.98m from the goal line

Centre spot – the place where a kick-off restarts the game, either after a goal or at the beginning of each half

Sideline

Pitch dimensions

Although pro pitches usually keep to the standard 100m-by-70m scale, a legal pitch can be anywhere between 91.4m and 118.8m long and 45.7m to 91.4m wide.

Centre circle – at kick-offs, opponents cannot enter this circle until the ball has been played

Player positions

Football started off simply with players being either forwards or backs. Now, with sweepers, midfield anchors, wing-backs and target men, player positions have become more complicated. That said, outfield players tend to be grouped into three categories – defenders, midfielders and attackers. Players' shirts are numbered to aid identification and, ever since the 1920s, teams have been asked to change into a second, or away, strip if their colours clash with those of the home side.

◄ Teams have a home strip and one or more away strips. These are Scottish club Celtic's home (top left) and away (left) shirts. Strips tend to change every season.

Ball in play

Ball in play

Ball out of play

Goal

No goal

No goal

No goal

In or out?

The ball is only out of play when it completely crosses the boundary lines of the pitch – including the goal line. A throw-in, goal kick, corner or goal is awarded depending on where the ball went out and which side last touched it. This applies to a ball in the air as well as one on the ground – so a clearance that curves over the sideline before landing in play will result in a throw-in to the opposition.

▶ *Luxembourg defender Jeff Strasser fails to prevent the ball crossing the line during a Euro 2000 qualifier.*

Halfway line – divides the pitch into two equal-sized areas of play. Players have to stay in their own half before a kick-off

Penalty arc – during a penalty kick, only the penalty taker is allowed in this space

Corner quadrant – corner kicks must be taken inside this area

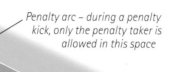

Penalty area – known as 'the box' and the area in which a keeper is allowed to handle the ball. Commit a foul in your box and your team could be facing a penalty

Goal line – if the ball completely crosses this line, a goal kick, corner or goal will be awarded

Goal area - known as the 'six-yard box' and the area in which goal kicks must be taken

▲ *This new stadium, which has an artificial surface, opened in Salzburg, Austria in 2003. It is one of four stadiums taking part in UEFA's experiments into possible replacements for turf.*

▼ *Norwegian groundsmen sweep the snow prior to Tromso's 1997 match with Chelsea.*

▲ *This 1995 match between Wimbledon and Blackburn Rovers was played in a mudbath at Selhurst Park stadium.*

The pitch

The rise of artificial turf in North America, and on training pitches all over the world, prompted ex-England manager Terry Venables to co-write a book entitled *They Used To Play On Grass*. Yet, a new century sees grass still king, even though it requires much care and preparation. A club or stadium's groundstaff are responsible for getting a pitch match-ready. Technical advances such as soil management and undersoil heating have helped reduce the number of games called off due to bad weather in many countries around the world.

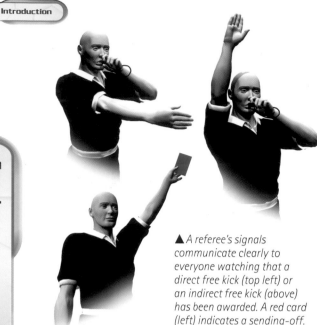

Key Rules

Knowing the laws of the game is not only part of becoming a footballer, it can also give you the edge in important matches. If you break the rules, you may forfeit your hard-earned possession of the ball and cost your team dear.

▲ A referee's signals communicate clearly to everyone watching that a direct free kick (top left) or an indirect free kick (above) has been awarded. A red card (left) indicates a sending-off.

Guardians of the game

Players should observe all the rules on the pitch, but in practice, it falls on the shoulders of the referee and his assistants to enforce the laws of the game. The officials make judgements on offsides, fouls and misconduct (see pages 14–15), whether the ball was in or out of play and if a handball has occurred. They have a range of signals at their disposal to communicate their decision to other officials, players and spectators.

▲ A corner kick is signalled clearly by the referee pointing to the corner flag.

▼ This referee is signalling for a goal kick to be taken from the goal area.

◄ The referee's assistant reinforces the referee's goal-kick signal by pointing his flag level with the front edge of the six-yard box.

▼ There are two stages to the signals for offside. First, the referee's assistant raises his flag upright to indicate that an offside has occurred. Following this, he angles his flag to show whether the offside occurred on the far side (1), centre (2) or near side (3) of the pitch.

▲ The assistant signals a throw-in, pointing a flag at the goal that the throwing-in team is attacking.

◄ The assistant signals for a corner and checks that the ball is placed within the quadrant by the corner-taker.

▲ The assistant signals that a substitution is about to take place.

Playing advantage

Referees have some flexibility in how they interpret the rules. A key part of this flexibility is the advantage rule. Playing advantage means that the referee has spotted a foul or infringement but, instead of awarding a free kick, he lets the game continue because it offers an advantage to the side sinned against. A good example of this is when an attacker is fouled but still manages to pass to a team-mate. Playing advantage reduces the number of interruptions and helps keep the game flowing.

▲ There's plenty of pressure on referees to get offside and other decisions right. Here, Swiss referee Urs Meier has to contend with players from the Turkish side, Galatasaray.

Offside

It's just one short football rule out of 17, yet more controversy is generated by Law 11 than any other. Offside is no evil plot to ruin football – it's actually in place to stop forwards goal-hanging (hanging around the goal, waiting to score) and helps generate exciting attacking and counter-attacking play. Much of the offside rule's bad press comes from its seeming complexity, yet the basic gist of the law is simple:

A player is offside when, at the moment the ball is played forward by a team-mate, the player is nearer to the opposition's goal line than both the ball and the second-from-last opponent.

A player cannot be offside in his own half of the pitch or when receiving the ball direct from a goal kick, corner or throw-in.

Examine these words. Opponents include the keeper as well as outfield players. If you're level with the second-from-last opposition player, be it a centre-back or the keeper rushing out, you're not offside. The 'at the moment the ball is played' part is vital, too. An essential part of attacking is to time runs so that you're onside as the ball is played ahead of you, yet can be behind defenders to collect the ball a split second later.

▲ When the ball was played is absolutely vital in an offside decision. Here, the player who scores is clearly in an offside position when the ball is played. His 'goal' is therefore disallowed as a result.

▲ The first attacker has foiled the onrushing goalkeeper by slipping the ball to a team-mate. With two defenders between the goalscorer and the goal, the player is onside, and the goal is allowed.

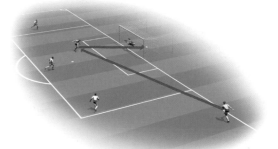

▲ You cannot be offside if you're behind the ball at the moment it is played. The scoring attacker only has the keeper in front of him. Yet, he is not offside, because the ball was cut back to him by his team-mate.

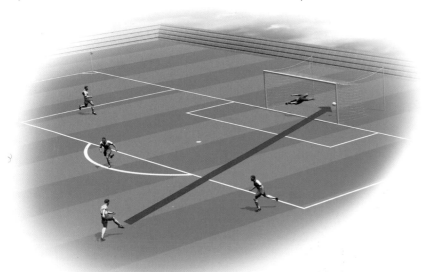

▲ Referees must judge if a player is interfering with or influencing play when offside. The player at the top left is offside but is not considered to be interfering or actively involved with play. The player who shoots is onside when he scores and the goal is given.

See also

12–13 Key Rules

54–55 Free Kicks

58–59 Penalty!

Fouls and Misconduct

Act against the spirit of the game or break its laws at your own peril. It's the referee's job to penalize actions such as shirt-pulling or tripping a player. If the offence is serious enough, you may be cautioned or even sent off.

Foul!

Tripping, pushing or holding back an opponent are just a few of the offences that are considered fouls. Depending on the offence and where it took place, the fouled-against team will be awarded a direct free kick, indirect free kick or penalty. Some free-kick offences, such as attempting to kick an opponent, apply even if the player fails to make contact. Offences resulting in an indirect free kick include time-wasting and obstruction. For a complete list of fouls, look at a copy of the laws of the game.

▼ *Thorsten Fink and Steve McManaman come to blows in a high-pressure Champions League semi-final encounter between Real Madrid and Bayern Munich.*

MASTERCLASS
Fouls and misconduct

Never argue with a referee. The referee's decision is final.

Never retaliate if you've been fouled. This is also a punishable offence.

Channel your aggression into winning the game, not attacking your opponents.

Always keep your cool and trust the officials to uphold the laws of the game.

No.1 Bobby Charlton

Some of the world's greatest footballers have also been the most well-behaved. During a career spanning more than 20 years and 860 club and country appearances, English footballer Bobby Charlton was never sent off.

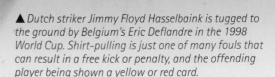

▲ *Dutch striker Jimmy Floyd Hasselbaink is tugged to the ground by Belgium's Eric Deflandre in the 1998 World Cup. Shirt-pulling is just one of many fouls that can result in a free kick or penalty, and the offending player being shown a yellow or red card.*

▼ Bologna's Nicola Boselli is guilty of dangerous play as he goes in high on Sporting Lisbon striker Leandro.

Booking

A booking, also known as a yellow card or a caution, sees the referee holding up a yellow card, and the player's name and shirt number being written down in the ref's book. Misconduct, including cynical, deliberate and dangerous play, is likely to see the referee reaching for the yellow card. Persistent minor infringements can also result in a booking.

Don't see red

Tempers often run high on the pitch but that's no excuse for a player to throw a punch or shout abuse at the officials. If you're guilty of any of these offences, or prevent a clear goal-scoring opportunity by fouling or handling the ball, you can expect a red card. Two yellow-card offences also mean an early bath. The red card is no badge of honour. Players who've been given their marching orders let their team down and give the opposition a big advantage. A sending-off can also result in a player being banned from playing in one or more games.

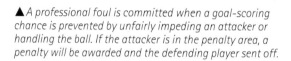

▲ A professional foul is committed when a goal-scoring chance is prevented by unfairly impeding an attacker or handling the ball. If the attacker is in the penalty area, a penalty will be awarded and the defending player sent off.

▼ Italian referee Pierluigi Collina is a familiar face in international football. He never shies away from tough decisions.

Under pressure

Refereeing is a tough job. Referees have to judge a fast-moving, dynamic game for 90 minutes or more. Decisions have to be made on the spot, and referees and their assistants don't have the benefit of slow-motion replays. Officials are only human and do make the occasional mistake. Even if you feel a referee has made a poor decision, do not challenge or try to change his or her mind. The referee's decision is always final.

▼ Officials can be subjected to verbal abuse and sometimes worse from a hostile crowd. The referee and his assistants in this Colombian domestic fixture are escorted off the pitch by riot police, protecting them from missiles thrown by spectators.

RED-CARD OFFENCES

A second cautionable offence

Using foul and abusive language

A professional foul

Violent conduct

Serious foul play such as deliberate handball

See also

10-11 Pitch and Players

60-61 Managers and Coaches

68-69 A Pro's Life

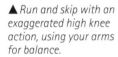

▲ This warm-up move involves performing a series of vigorous star jumps to get the blood circulating.

▲ Run and skip with an exaggerated high knee action, using your arms for balance.

▲ This exercise involves jogging along with a high backlift so that your heels almost touch your bottom.

Ready to Play

With seconds to go before the ref blows the whistle and the match starts, the tension is mounting. Are you ready for the game – really ready? Have you stretched and warmed up properly? Is your kit in good order and have you drunk enough water?

Warm-up act

Being prepared for a match involves far more than packing a spare set of socks, crossing your fingers and jogging out onto the pitch. Players of all ages and abilities need to warm up and get their bodies in gear for the game. Warming up can involve activities such as jogging round the pitch, some short sprints, and star jumps, among other routines. Teams that have warmed-up properly may have an advantage over their opponents, allowing them to react more quickly in the opening minutes.

Stretching

Football can push your body to the limit, and stretching the muscles before a match allows them to work at their peak, improving performance and reducing injuries. Warm up before stretching and always ease gently into and out of a stretch – never stretch too far. Hold each stretch position for five to ten seconds and repeat the stretch several times.

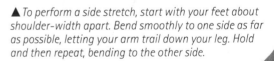

▲ To perform a side stretch, start with your feet about shoulder-width apart. Bend smoothly to one side as far as possible, letting your arm trail down your leg. Hold and then repeat, bending to the other side.

▲ For floor splits, push your head down towards each knee and the ground, holding for five seconds.

▼ Perform this thigh stretch after the other stretches. Using one hand for support, pull back your leg smoothly. Hold for ten seconds, then repeat with the other leg.

▲ Sitting down with the soles of your feet pressed together, use your elbows to push your knees down, and hold the position to stretch your groin muscles.

▼ ▶ Alessandro Del Piero's silver boots (below) feature studs moulded into the sole of the boot. Many boots come with replaceable screw-in studs (right).

Boot camp

First and foremost, your boots must be a comfortable fit. Don't squeeze your foot into a size too small or let it roam about in a size too large just because it's endorsed by your favourite player. Figo, Zidane or Rivaldo's footwear isn't going to transform you into these heroes. Forget the logos and the hype – a pair of boots that fits well, and is well-made and looked after, is all that you need.

Good boots are made of soft leather to let your foot 'feel' the ball – regular cleaning and polishing will help keep the leather soft. Good boots are also flexible, should offer you plenty of support around the ankle and have a wide tongue that won't slip to one side or the other. When your boots get wet, allow them to dry naturally instead of in front of a heat source, otherwise the leather might crack. Help them keep their shape by stuffing them with newspaper after wear.

Shirts, shorts and shinpads

Cotton shirts and shorts have been largely replaced by man-made materials. Tucking your shirt into your shorts isn't just about looking smart – it gives opponents less material to grab. Socks can be held up with small strips of material called 'ties'. In earlier times, sliding newspapers down the front of your socks was the only protection against a crack across the shins. Today's shinpads are usually made of a light plastic, but can save you from a bruising.

▼ Professional players, such as Saudi Arabian international Sami Al Jaber who is pictured here, warm up and stretch thoroughly before training or prior to a match.

▲ Unlike early footballs (above), today's balls are light in weight and waterproof, like the Adidas Finale ball (top).

▲ Shinpads are compulsory at all levels of the modern game. Get used to shinpads by wearing them in training and practice matches.

▼ Drinking small amounts of liquids such as water or flat, fruit-juice-based drinks, before, during and after a training session or match is essential.

▲ The heavy cotton shirts of yesteryear (left) have largely been replaced by clothing manufactured from lighter man-made materials (right).

MASTERCLASS
Ready to play

Take warming up seriously even if team-mates don't.

Remember to ease your way gently through a stretch.

Clean and look after your kit – it will last longer that way.

Wear a tracksuit before a game to keep warm and regularly drink small amounts of water.

▲ The German national side, like all teams, keep warm in training and before a match by wearing tracksuits and other training clothing.

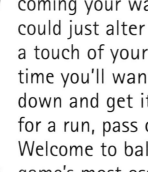

◀ For side-foot cushioning, get into position early with your weight on your standing foot. Watch the ball onto your foot, then bring your foot back slightly to pull the ball down.

▲ Use the underside of your boot to trap the ball. Bring your foot down firmly, but don't stamp on the ball – it may pop out from under your control.

Ball Control

A long ball from a team-mate is coming your way. Although you could just alter its direction with a touch of your foot, most of the time you'll want to slow the ball down and get it at your feet, ready for a run, pass or a shot at goal. Welcome to ball control – one of the game's most essential group of skills.

The soft option

Damping and killing are terms often used to describe stopping the pace and direction of a ball. What you're actually doing is cushioning the ball. This involves following the direction of the ball with the part of your body that makes contact with it. Whichever part of your body you use for cushioning, try to stay relaxed and balanced, watching the ball very closely and moving as smoothly as possible.

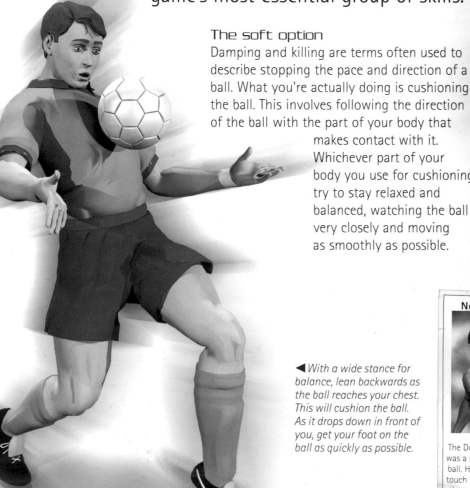

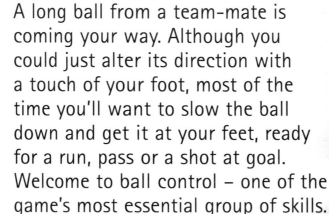

◀ With a wide stance for balance, lean backwards as the ball reaches your chest. This will cushion the ball. As it drops down in front of you, get your foot on the ball as quickly as possible.

No.2 Ruud Gullit

The Dutch player Ruud Gullit was a superb controller of the ball. He had a wonderful first touch that gave him plenty of time and room to deploy his other formidable skills.

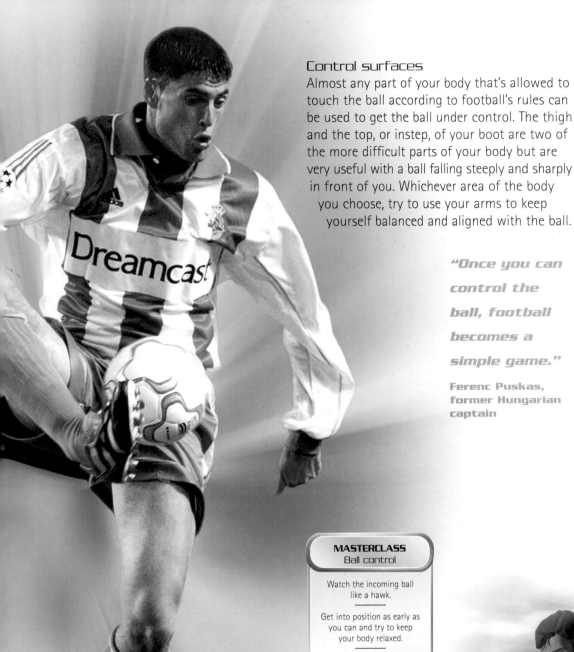

Control surfaces

Almost any part of your body that's allowed to touch the ball according to football's rules can be used to get the ball under control. The thigh and the top, or instep, of your boot are two of the more difficult parts of your body but are very useful with a ball falling steeply and sharply in front of you. Whichever area of the body you choose, try to use your arms to keep yourself balanced and aligned with the ball.

"Once you can control the ball, football becomes a simple game."

Ferenc Puskas, former Hungarian captain

▲ *The instep cushion requires you to get your foot up, with the instep facing the ball, and toe pointing slightly down. As the ball arrives, bring your foot down with the ball nestling just above it.*

MASTERCLASS
Ball control

Watch the incoming ball like a hawk.

Get into position as early as you can and try to keep your body relaxed.

Just before impact, move the cushioning part of your body in the direction of the ball's flight.

Try to set the ball down as close as possible to your feet.

◀ *Deportivo la Coruna star Diego Tristan, under pressure from Paris SG's Frederic Dehu, times his jump to meet and cushion a rising ball with his foot.*

▶ *For the thigh cushion, the upper part of your leg should be almost parallel with the pitch. Pull your leg down and back as the ball makes contact. This will kill the ball's pace and should leave it in front of you.*

Practise, practise, practise

Don't wait until your side's next training session, get out there and practise your ball-control skills whenever you can. Work with a friend and pass the ball to each other at different speeds and heights. On your own? No problem. Find an outside wall in a safe place and bounce a ball off it at varying angles to practise the full range of cushioning skills.

See also

22–23 Advanced Passing | 24–25 Movement and Space | 26–27 On-ball Skills | 42–43 Attacking Skills

Passing

Passing glues together a team's play, turns defence into attack, switches the direction of play and creates goalscoring opportunities. When you make a pass, you have to decide where and to whom to pass, when to release the ball and which type of pass to make.

▲ *Pinpoint sidefoot passes can be made on the move as Fulham's Margunn Haugenes shows.*

Accuracy and weight

Accuracy is the key to good passing. The ball needs to travel in the direction that you want without it being intercepted by the opposition. Your pass also needs to reach its destination in a way that makes it easy for the receiver to control. An important factor is the speed, or pace, with which the ball leaves your foot. This is also known as the weight of a pass and it depends on how far back you take your kicking foot and how fast you bring your foot through the ball. Only experience teaches you how to vary the weight of a pass.

"I was right-footed to start with, but I worked harder on my left and it became better than my right." George Best

◀ *Sweden's Karolina Westberg has the ball under control at her feet, ready to make a pass. She is in a good position to pass the ball with the outside of her foot or to make an instep pass (see below).*

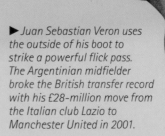

1   2   3

▲ *You can use different parts of your foot to make a pass. The most common are the inside of your foot (1), which will give you most control, the outside of your foot (2) and the instep (3) – the part of your foot where the bootlaces are found.*

▶ *Juan Sebastian Veron uses the outside of his boot to strike a powerful flick pass. The Argentinian midfielder broke the British transfer record with his £28-million move from the Italian club Lazio to Manchester United in 2001.*

1   2   3

▲ *Striking the middle of the ball with a smooth follow-through keeps the ball low as it travels over the pitch. This makes it easier for a team-mate to receive and control. Sidefoot passes are especially useful up to distances of approximately 20m.*

Sidefoot passing

The sidefoot, or push, pass uses the inside of the foot to strike the ball, keeping it close to the ground. You'll really feel in control with this pass because a large portion of the foot makes contact with the ball, making it easier to direct the ball precisely where you want it. Your non-kicking foot should be close to the ball and point in the direction of the pass. With your body over the ball and your eyes focussed on it, swing your leg from your hip through the ball. Keep your ankle firm as you make impact and aim to hit the ball through its centre.

▲ *Real Madrid's Fernando Redondo displays textbook positioning and balance as he makes a sidefoot pass.*

No.3 Hidetoshi Nakata

A superb passer of the ball, Japanese midfielder Hidetoshi Nakata was voted 1998 Asian Player of the Year and has starred in Italy's Serie A for Perugia and Roma.

▼ *Make a gate with two cones or other objects that are between 60–80cm apart. Pass the ball through the gate. Gradually, stand further away and shrink the gate size to work on passing accuracy.*

Passing drill

Top footballers never give up honing their passing skills. Take passing practices as seriously as the professionals. Aim for quick control and crisp, accurate passes to the receiver. The biggest single improvement you can bring to your game is to become a fully two-footed player. To do this, you'll need to work especially hard on your weaker foot in practices and training sessions. Ask your coach for a range of different passing drills so that you don't get bored performing the same exercises every time you're training.

MASTERCLASS
Passing

Keep your head still and your eyes focussed on the ball as you make the pass.

Aim to strike the ball with the correct amount of weight.

Move as soon as you've made the pass.

Build up passing skills with your weaker foot and practise as often as possible.

See also

20-21 Passing

26-27 On-ball Skills

36-37 Fancy Skills

Advanced Passing

Players with a wide range of different passing techniques at their disposal often control and dictate a match. While the sidefoot pass is the most frequently used, other passing techniques allow you to hit a bouncing ball, to chip the ball or to make very long passes.

◄When under pressure, select a target and type of pass that you can execute accurately and quickly. Here, the player hits a sidefoot pass.

▲A chip pass will carry the ball over the heads of your opponents. Aim to strike the bottom of the ball with a downwards stab and a short follow-through. Your boot and the ground act as a wedge, forcing the ball up at a steep angle.

Timing

If the player you're passing to is on the move, you'll need to calculate where this team-mate will be when the pass reaches his or her feet. Aim for this spot, not where your team-mate is positioned when you strike the ball. Even with a relatively short pass, the player receiving the ball might have run forwards several metres.

◄ The compass drill is a good way of sharpening your passing skills. As the ball is passed, a player shouts North, South, East or West. The player in the centre then has to turn and pass the ball in that direction.

Instep drive

The instep pass, or drive, allows you to hit longer passes when you're either still or on the move. With arms out for balance, non-kicking foot next to the ball and your body over the ball, swing your kicking leg back then forward with your toes pointing to the ground. Your boot laces should make contact with the middle of the ball. The follow-through should be long and smooth. By changing the angle of your foot and body as well as the length of your backswing, you can make passes of different height and length.

► Spanish player Gaizka Mendieta completes a lofted instep drive. His body is upright and the follow-through takes his kicking leg across his body.

▲ A lofted instep drive will take the ball quickly through the air. To make this kind of pass, plant the non-kicking foot behind and to the side of the ball. You'll need to strike the lower half of the ball and, on the follow-through, your leg should swing across your body.

"Football is a simple game based on the giving and taking of passes." **Bill Shankly**

Flick passes

You'll often receive the ball under great pressure, with opponents closing in on you. Inside and outside flick passes are ideal when time and space is limited. Flicks are short passes along or just above the ground. Use the toe end of your boot in a short but firm flicking movement. If you're under extreme pressure, you can also use your toe and lower laces of your instep to flick the ball right back to the player who has just passed the ball to you.

> **MASTERCLASS**
> Advanced passing
>
> Use the instep drive for longer passing.
>
> Try to keep your body between opponents and the ball as you release a pass.
>
> When making shorter passes, especially in crowded areas, use the sidefoot pass

◄ In tight situations such as this, you can use the outside of the foot to perform a flick pass. Try to make contact with the ball using the little toe area of your boot.

See also

20-21 Passing

26-27 On-ball Skills

42-43 Attacking Skills

Movement and Space

Movement and awareness of space are vital components of any good passing team and will allow you to 'let the ball do the work'. Crisp, accurate passing together with decisive movement into space can get the ball around a pitch much faster than a single player or covering defenders can travel. Precise passing and movement can open up even the tightest of defences.

▲ *Practise passing in triangles with players interchanging positions, keeping relatively close to each other (but less than 10 to 12m) as they move around the pitch.*

▲ *Mark out a small area with cones. Three players should try to keep possession of the ball from a defender by passing and moving. If the defender gets the ball or it goes out of play, he should switch places with one of the other three.*

Pass and move

Don't rest on your laurels and stand still after delivering a pass. Get moving and look to support the player who now has the ball. Alert players seek to get themselves quickly into a position to receive the ball again or into space for the second, third or fourth pass in a move. By acting quickly after making a pass, you can wrongfoot defenders and open up play.

MASTERCLASS
Movement and space

With or without the ball, always keep your head up, looking for opportunities to move into space.

Be aware of the positions of opponents, team-mates and the player with the ball.

Football is fast-moving. Space that was there the last time you looked, may have gone. Other space may have opened up elsewhere. Check first.

No.5 Enzo Scifo

Belgian legend Enzo Scifo was both masterful at passing and excellent at support play, seemingly able always to find good positions in which to receive the ball.

Be a space invader

The football pitch is a big place. Even with a full complement of players, pockets of space still exist. It's these that you should be looking for and moving into. Not having the ball is no reason to relax – it's quite the opposite. Use the time to search for space in a good position, invade the space and look to receive a pass. Football is a dynamic game with opportunities opening up or closing remarkably quickly. Look not just for space but areas that aren't blocked off by defenders – positions that offer the on-ball player a clear, safe path to pass to you.

▼ The 'push and go' calls for a weighted pass that travels past a defender's legs and allows you to run onto it quickly. Start sprinting as soon as the ball leaves your foot.

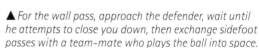

Slipping markers

A player looking to receive the ball must sometimes shake off a defender who is marking him closely. Jogging around from place to place aimlessly just won't do. Make life hard for the defender with sudden changes of pace or direction – fake a move away from your target space, then turn quickly and sprint into it to trick a marker.

▼ Luis Figo's superb ball skills are shown to good effect as he starts to perform an outside hook turn.

▲ Inside hook – lean into the direction you want to turn and hook the inside of your foot right around the ball, dragging it with you as you turn and move away.

▲ Outside hook – leaning in the direction you want to turn, reach across your body with that side's foot. Hook the outside of your foot around the ball and sweep it away as you turn.

▲ For the wall pass, approach the defender, wait until he attempts to close you down, then exchange sidefoot passes with a team-mate who plays the ball into space.

Space behind opponents

A key area to be aware of and look to exploit is the space behind a nearby opponent. The opponent is guarding an area of the pitch, so getting past him can open up opportunities. Dribbling and turning (see On-ball Skills, pages 26–27) can get you past but so can other, less-fancy, techniques. One move is the wall, or return pass, for which you pass to a team-mate then receive it straight back on the other side of a defender. Another is the more risky 'push and go', which sees you approach a defender, push the ball past him to one side and run onto collect it. The defender has to turn while you're heading the right way.

Turning

Changing direction with the ball is an important part of your game. In busy areas of the pitch, look to turn and change direction as soon as you receive a pass and have the ball under control. This often outwits opponents and buys you precious time to look up and make a pass or shot, or set out on a run. Always keep yourself between the ball and opponents when making a turn, and swivel on one foot using the other to move the ball either with sidefoot or instep nudges, if in plenty of space, or by using an outside or inside hook, if under pressure.

On-ball Skills

Running with the ball, protecting it from opponents, and dribbling are all techniques and skills that require good ball control and excellent awareness of the game around you.

◀ Nigerian star Jay-Jay Okocha shows good awareness as he races forwards, with the ball in constant reach.

Moving with the ball

If you have the ball and see a large, promising area of space ahead, move into it as quickly as possible. You must kick the ball far enough to allow you to maintain a good running speed but not so far that you lose control and, worse, possession of the ball. Using the outside of the foot allows you to keep moving at speed. When running with the ball, you need eyes everywhere, so keep glancing up at the game around you, and down at the position of the ball.

▲ Shielding requires some strength, but mostly you need skill and an ability to watch out for opponents.

◀ Spanish striker Raul displays excellent shielding technique as Slovenia's Darko Milanic seeks to make a challenge.

▲ This player has the ball under control and has turned his body to shield the ball from his opponent.

MASTERCLASS
On-ball skills

Good balance, shielding and awareness are needed when on the ball.

Think about the result of your on-ball move – where, when and to whom are you going to pass?

One-on-one drills and small-sided games are the places to hone your on-ball skills.

Always look for the simple option.

▲ The player now has a little more time to choose his next move, which is a lay-off sidefoot pass.

Shielding

Shielding, or screening, is a valuable way of keeping control of the ball and preventing opponents from stealing possession. It involves you putting your body between opponent and ball and keeping it there legally, even if that means staying aware of your opponent's moves and shifting position. The difference between shielding the ball and impeding another player largely comes down to whether or not you have the ball under control. You cannot just block the path of an opponent or push or hold onto him. As soon as you start shielding, you should be keeping the ball under control and thinking about your next step. This is most likely to be a pass to an unmarked team-mate, although it can be a much fancier, and riskier, move such as a hook and turn (see page 25) around the opposition player.

▲ The player running and dribbling the ball is about to be closed down by a defender. The dribbler drops his right shoulder and leans a little in one direction.

Dribbling

A skill guaranteed to get crowds on their feet, dribbling calls for good balance, superb control and plenty of confidence. Keep the ball in front of you and close to your feet but never under them or you may overrun the ball. You can use your instep, and the outside and inside of your foot, to nudge the ball forward and to each side. Dribbling is a high-risk move and even the very best players surrender the ball on occasion. This is why you should only dribble when away from your defensive third of the pitch and always be on the lookout for a safe pass. A good dribbler knows where he is heading and when to release the ball, and how to avoid getting cornered by two or three defenders.

▲ Practise dribbling at walking pace, then build up your speed. Using slalom courses can help you to keep your balance and control while changing direction, as this Fulham youth player demonstrates.

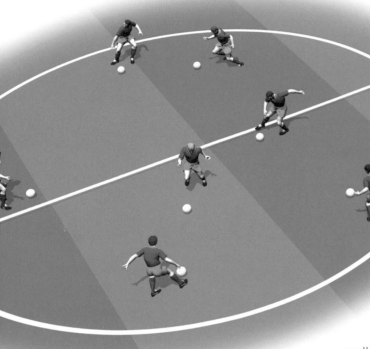

▲ For this dribble and tag game, each player is given a ball and must stay within the centre circle. If you touch a player with your hand, gain a point. If you are tagged, lose a point, and if you lose control of the ball or dribble outside the circle, forfeit two points.

Dribbling deception

Unless you're blessed with outstanding pace, dribbling without deception is a surefire way of losing the ball. Deception can take the form of tricks such as feinting – pretending to move past an opponent in one direction, only to go the other way – or sudden changes in pace, from sprint to walk to sprint again. Feinting requires exaggeration and confidence to really sell the defender the notion that you will head left, when you intend to go right. In all deception moves, accelerate away from the opponent you have just deceived, keeping yourself between the ball and player as much as possible.

▲ The body movement by the dribbler tricks the defender into believing his opponent is going to head one way. The defender commits himself to that direction.

▲ As the defender commits himself to the wrong direction, the on-ball player is able to swerve around his opponent in the opposite direction and dribble away.

No.6 Harry Kewell

With the ball seemingly stuck to his feet at times, Australian Harry Kewell terrifies defences. But Kewell also knows when to release the ball, either with a telling pass or a deadly shot.

See also

46–47 Defending

48–49 Defending as a Unit

1   2   3   4

▲ *For the front-block tackle, the tackler (in white) approaches the on-ball player (1), getting his bodyweight over his foot and striking the ball firmly (2). The tackler concentrates on dispossessing his opponent (3), before moving away quickly with the ball under control (4).*

Tackling

When the opposition has the ball, there are a number of ways to win it back. You can try to intercept a pass, or you can make a challenge for the ball with a tackle. Although tackling can leave you open to being dribbled around, it is a key part of your game. Tackling isn't just for defenders, it's a skill required all over the pitch.

▲ *This ill-timed lunge from behind doesn't make contact with the ball and so is a foul. The player may be booked or sent off, and a free kick or penalty will be awarded to the opposition depending on where the foul was committed.*

The front-block tackle

The block tackle is the most commonly used tackle. For this tackle, you'll usually be facing an opponent from the front. Plant your non-tackling foot firmly on the ground and lean forward into the tackle. This will give you a solid base. Use the inside of your foot to make strong, firm contact with the middle of the ball. Often, this will be enough to remove the ball from your opponent.

No.7 Franco Baresi

Franco Baresi, one of Italy's finest-ever sweepers, was a superb tackler. Along with Marco Van Basten and Ruud Gullit he played a major role in AC Milan's successes.

Tackling tips

The timing of a tackle really comes only with experience and practice. Try to make your move when your opponent is unbalanced, looking down at the ball or playing it too far in front. Aim to tackle from the front or side, staying on your feet whenever possible. This lets you come away with the ball or, if you're unsuccessful in the tackle, to chase after the ball. Determination and confidence are very important – if you don't fully commit yourself to a tackle, your challenge is probably going to fail and you are more likely to hurt yourself.

Sliding tackle

Sliding tackles are sometimes the only way to deflect or clear a ball. Although sliding tackles look spectacular, if they're executed badly there can be a high risk of injury or being penalized with a free kick or penalty. Make sure you bend your supporting leg at the knee as you slide in on it. As you make contact with the ball, you need to transfer your bodyweight to your tackling leg and foot. Although they usually just clear the ball, some tacklers try to hook their foot around the ball to keep possession.

◄ Sometimes, players have to challenge when the ball is in mid-air. Here, England's Karen Burke and Scotland's Michelle Barr compete for the ball.

MASTERCLASS
Tackling

Always go for the ball, never the player.

During a tackle, watch the ball, not your opponent.

Stand firm in block tackles, using your weight to make the tackle.

Once the tackle is made, get the ball under control, keep your head up and start moving.

► Tottenham defender Sol Campbell times his sliding tackle to perfection as he wins the ball from Arsenal player Robert Pires. In 2001, Campbell left Spurs to link up with Pires at Arsenal.

▲ England midfielder Steven Gerrard challenges Brazilian striker Rivaldo from the side. He gets his weight on the tackling leg and bends the supporting one for extra stability as he makes the tackle.

See also

36-37 Fancy Skills

42-43 Attacking Skills

44-45 Opening up Defences

Volleying and Shooting

To get the ball past the goalkeeper and any defenders, your shot has to be struck with the right combination of power and accuracy. When the ball is off the ground, you'll need to make a volley. As well as attempts on goal, volleys can also be used for quick passes and long clearances.

No.8 Marco Van Basten

Dutch centre-forward Marco Van Basten was a magnificent striker of the ball, with some spectacular goals to his credit. These include a memorable volley against the USSR in the 1988 European Championships.

The volley

A volley is made when the foot and ball connect in mid-air. Because you can get the full weight of your body into a volley, it's one of the most powerful shots you can make. When a volleyed shot comes off, it can be spectacular but you'll need to keep your eye on the ball and accurately judge its pace as it comes towards you.

▲ Volleys can be used in both attacking and defensive situations. Here, French central defender Marcel Desailly performs a clearance volley to get the ball out of danger.

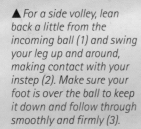

▲ For a side volley, lean back a little from the incoming ball (1) and swing your leg up and around, making contact with your instep (2). Make sure your foot is over the ball to keep it down and follow through smoothly and firmly (3).

Sidefoot volleying

Using the side of your foot, you can perform two types of volley. The first is a gentle, slightly cushioned pass to a nearby team-mate who is in a better position. This is called a lay-off volley. You'll need to meet the ball early and your foot should make contact with the middle, or just above the middle, of the ball. The sidefoot volley can also be used as a close-range shot to steer a bouncing ball towards the goal.

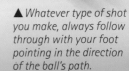

▲ Whatever type of shot you make, always follow through with your foot pointing in the direction of the ball's path.

1   2   3

◄ For a front-on instep volley, prepare to lift your knee, and point your toes downwards (1). Keep your head in front of the knee of your kicking leg (2). Look for a clean contact to send the ball in the direction you want (3).

Shot placement

The instep drive is the basis of the shooting technique you'll most frequently use. Unlike using the instep for a long, lofted pass, the key to shooting is to get your body over the ball and to keep the shot low. If you have the time and space to pick an exact place to shoot, aim low into the corners of the goal. It takes a goalkeeper longer to dive low than to dive and stretch high. If you're to one side of the goal, try to aim for the corner of the goal not covered by the keeper.

▲ For a half volley, the ball should be hit as soon as it touches the ground. Stretch your ankle so your toes point downwards and keep your knees bent.

▶ English legend Dixie Dean, who scored 60 goals for Everton in the 1927–28 season, lines up a shot using the instep drive to power the ball forwards.

Shot selection

Long-range shots require a volley or instep drive to generate enough power to trouble the goalkeeper. If you have learned how to bend or swerve the ball, you'll be even more effective. From short range, many players prefer accuracy over power and hit the ball firmly with the sidefoot. If the goalkeeper has advanced off the goal line, a chip kick or lob may be the best shot to make.

▲ Marked-out squares on a wall make excellent targets for shooting practice. One player passes the ball and calls out a square, which the other player then attempts to hit.

▲ Japan's Naohira Takahar plays a lob volley in an attempt to lift the ball over the Uruguayan goalkeeper.

See also

42-43 Attacking Skills

44-45 Opening up Defences

46-47 Defending

52-53 The Corner Kick

Heading

A football can spend as much time in the air as on the pitch, so heading is a skill that all players, not just central defenders and strikers, need. Heading doesn't hurt – or rather, it shouldn't. Heading is painless, as long as you use your forehead to make contact with the ball.

▲ A power header from a running position involves a player leaping off his front foot to create maximum thrust as the ball is met. Bending the knees helps to keep the player balanced on landing.

▲ Aim to hit the ball with your forehead. Remember to try to keep your eyes open until after contact.

▲ Corner kicks often create good heading opportunities. Excellent control is needed to guide the ball away from the goalkeeper's hands.

Eyes wide open

Usually, when you make a header you'll be directing the ball horizontally or downwards. Try not to shut your eyes as you meet the ball but watch it right onto your forehead. Your body position should allow you to get over the ball. The exception to this is when clearing a ball from defence. In this instance, you still need to use your forehead but position yourself under the ball to send it forwards and upwards.

Meeting the ball

Only jump to head the ball when absolutely necessary. Heading with your feet on the ground gives you a more stable, balanced base. Try to get into position early and meet the ball, rather than just let the ball hit your head. You also need to keep your neck muscles taut just before you make contact, in order to support your head and provide maximum control.

▶ The Danish midfielder Allan Nielsen makes a spectacular diving header for Tottenham Hotspur against Coventry City. Note how his arms are extended to help break his fall.

Power heading

To put more force into a header, arch your back and thrust your upper body and head forwards and through the ball. For even more pace and distance, you can spring off the ground to meet the ball in mid-air. Timing is essential. Ideally, you want to connect with the ball at the top of your jump. You can generate extra force by driving your arms backwards to help propel your head firmly through the ball.

No.9 Ivan Zamorano

At a far-from-towering 1.78m, Chilean striker Ivan Zamorano has proved for many years that you don't have to be the tallest player on the pitch to be an excellent header of the ball.

▲ *French defender Laurent Blanc makes a header upfield. Defenders like Blanc who are very good in the air often join the attack at set pieces such as free kicks or corners.*

Other headers

The cushioning header is similar to the basic header but, as the ball reaches your forehead, you should recoil smoothly back and down, killing the pace of the ball and leaving it at your feet. The flick-on header tends to be used from a long clearance, a nearpost corner kick or a goal kick from your keeper. Flick the ball behind you, hopefully in the direction of a strike partner. It is one of the most difficult headers to master.

▼ *Defensive headers require both height and distance. Here, the defender meets the ball at the top of his jump and angles his head to clear the danger.*

▲ *This effective heading drill begins with one player using an underarm throw to lob the ball at headable height to a partner five metres away. The header should be aimed down towards the thrower's feet for him to practise ball control. After ten headers, swop roles.*

MASTERCLASS
Heading

Don't be scared of the ball.

Make sure your body is both balanced and relaxed.

If you can, keep your eyes open while heading the ball.

When jumping to head the ball, you can use your arms for balance but keep your elbows down to avoid fouls or injuries.

See also

20–21 Passing

24–25 Movement and Space

30–31 Volleying and Shooting

▲▶ *Footballers of all ages and skill levels can take part in and enjoy small-sided games, as these former stars, playing in a veterans' five-a-side tournament, illustrate.*

Small-sided Games

Playing small-sided games is not only fun, it can also help improve your skills for regular matches. Millions of people play small-sided games during their breaks from work, in fun after-school sessions and in competitive evening and weekend leagues.

Why smaller games?

In 11-a-side matches, you may feel uninvolved and far from the action for long periods of the game. A big advantage of small-sided contests is that they simply don't allow you to hide for long. Players see plenty of the ball, have to make more touches and playmaking decisions and will practise certain skills and techniques more than they would in a regular game of football. There are also far fewer stoppages and less reliance on set pieces in smaller-sided games. This forces players to be constantly prepared for action.

▼▶ *Five-a-side has different rules to the regular game. Playing the ball over head height (right) and entering the keeper's area (below) are both banned.*

Walled five-a-side

Five-a-side games allow players of all ages to compete in indoor or outdoor matches, from informal lunchtime sessions to seriously contested leagues. Five-a-side rules vary but usually ban the ball from travelling above shoulder or head height and outfield players from entering the goalkeeper's area. Many pitches feature low-height goals, and walls in place of touchlines. These help keep the ball in play and encourage footballers to play passes off the walls to beat opponents.

▶ *The walls surrounding five-a-side pitches offer a handy way of beating opponents. Here, the on-ball player's path to the left and straight ahead is blocked. He opts to play the ball against the wall, running around the other side of his opponent to collect it.*

Small-sided games for young players

More and more youth and children's coaches are turning to small-sided games as a key way of fast-tracking young players' skills. Small-sided contests place a premium on technique and movement, not height or physique, and so are ideal for players who are still growing. There aren't the large pitches or strict team formations found in the full-sized game so everyone gets the chance to hone their attacking and defending skills. Small-sided matches encourage attacking play. Players learn that a two or more goal deficit can be overcome quickly with fast, precise passing as well as movement and low shots. The quick pace of the action also means there's no chance to brood over mistakes.

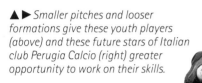

▲▶ *Smaller pitches and looser formations give these youth players (above) and these future stars of Italian club Perugia Calcio (right) greater opportunity to work on their skills.*

Futsal

Futsal is a form of five-a-side football approved by FIFA in 1989 and played increasingly all over the world. There are no walls around the edge of the pitch, and the junior-sized ball can travel above head height. Played on a roughly basketball-sized court and with rolling substitutes, Futsal games are two halves of 20 minutes, but the clock is stopped whenever the ball goes out of play. One rule states that if a team makes six serious fouls in one half, the ref will award a direct free kick no more than 12m from goal, with no defensive wall allowed.

◀▲ *Small-sided games can be played in a wide variety of locations. This inflatable court allows five-a-side action to spring up almost anywhere.*

▲ *This picture is from a recreation ground in Buenos Aires, Argentina but there are similar sights in parks, gardens and areas of open land all over the world. Players look to improve their skills with simple kickabout matches, playing keeping the ball up or games of headers and volleys.*

On the streets

Football can be played almost anywhere as long as it is away from traffic, windows and other hazards. All top footballers can fondly recall practising either on their own or with a few friends in the streets, gardens and parks of their towns or cities. Many pros believe that their superb close skills came from kicking around a tennis or other small ball. The smaller ball demands excellent touch and close control.

Beach football

Beach football is a fun and popular pastime played by many that has recently grown into an organized sport. It features a number of prestigious tournaments, including Umbro's Pro Beach Soccer series, starring players who were formerly top internationals on grass such as Italy's Lodovico Costacurta, Portugal's Adelino Nunes and England's John Barnes.

◀▼ *Many stars, such as Claudio Gentile of Italy (among those pictured left), now play in beach football tournaments. Brazilian maestro Zico (below) grew up playing Futsal and credits this for developing his remarkable skills.*

See also

30-31 Volleying and Shooting

34-35 Small-sided Games

"Football is about glory... doing things in style... doing them with a flourish."

Danny Blanchflower

Fancy Skills

Spectacular overhead kicks, aerial side volleys, lobs from the halfway line – all breathtaking to watch, especially when executed by a Best or a Pelé or a Figo. You are more likely to make use of slightly less ambitious but extremely valuable skills such as the backheel pass or dragback.

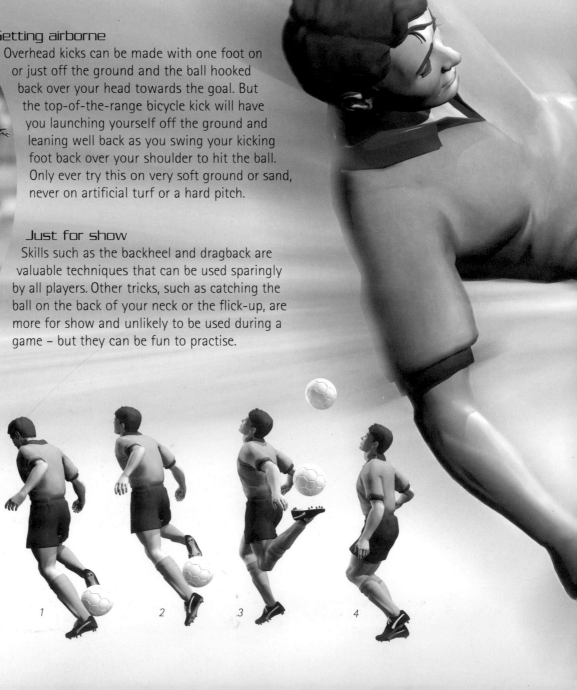

◀ *The backheel is a good way of changing the direction of the ball and fooling your opponents. With your non-kicking foot level with the ball, strike through the centre of the ball with your heel or the sole of your boot.*

◀ *An aerial side volley is a spectacular way of dealing with a high, rising ball.*

Getting airborne

Overhead kicks can be made with one foot on or just off the ground and the ball hooked back over your head towards the goal. But the top-of-the-range bicycle kick will have you launching yourself off the ground and leaning well back as you swing your kicking foot back over your shoulder to hit the ball. Only ever try this on very soft ground or sand, never on artificial turf or a hard pitch.

Just for show

Skills such as the backheel and dragback are valuable techniques that can be used sparingly by all players. Other tricks, such as catching the ball on the back of your neck or the flick-up, are more for show and unlikely to be used during a game – but they can be fun to practise.

▲ *Clever Chala of Ecuador performs an excellent overhead kick. He gets his foot over the ball to keep the ball's height down.*

▶ *For the flick-up, place one foot in front of the ball and trap it between the toes of your back foot and the heel of the front (1). Lift your back foot up to roll the ball over your heel (2), then flick the ball up (3) and over your head (4) so that it lands at your feet.*

1   2   3   4

You've been nutmegged

Few things are more embarrassing for a player than being 'nutmegged'. A nutmeg means putting the ball through the open legs of an opponent, either for a team-mate to receive the pass on the other side or for you to run around the startled, nutmegged player and collect the ball. Nutmegs are risky but when they come off they can be effective.

1

2

3

4

▲ *Faouzi Rouissi of Tunisia (left) nutmegs Congo's Kibemba Mbayo (right), playing the ball straight through his legs.*

Self-restraint

Although you can practise fancy tricks such as overhead kicks to sharpen your skills and to impress your friends, you probably won't have many opportunities to use them in a real game. Only use these skills when it gives your team an advantage – rather than simply for the entertainment of other players and spectators.

No.10 Rivaldo

The Brazilian player Rivaldo has a dazzling array of skills. They've helped the midfielder become the top scorer in the Spanish League and won him FIFA's World Player of the Year.

▼ *Zinedine Zidane (below right) displays his brilliant ball control skills, using the outside of his foot to take the ball down while on the move.*

▲ *The dragback is a good way of wrongfooting an opponent. You look as if you're going to play the ball in one direction but instead you stop the ball (1), drag it back (2), and pivot (3), before moving off in another direction (4).*

◄ *USA's Claudio Reyna balances a ball on his head during a practice session.*

▲ *Colombia's maverick goalkeeper René Higuita has a novel method of clearing the ball from his goal area. This technique, which involves flicking his feet over the back of his head, has been dubbed the 'scorpion kick'.*

► *Drills in which players stand a short distance away from the keeper and kick or throw the ball at varying heights and speeds make vital practice routines.*

"The goalie has to be one of the fittest, most agile, quick-thinking and determined players in the team." Gordon Banks

Goalkeeping Basics

Goalkeeping is a unique skill and one that carries a lot of responsibility. The only player allowed to handle the ball – inside his penalty area – a goalkeeper is the last line of defence. A sloppy goalkeeping performance can lose the better side a game whereas an inspired performance can secure a memorable win. More hinges on the goalie than any other single player.

▲ *Swedish keeper Magnus Hedman shows a good stance from which he can make any goalkeeping move.*

Stance

Maintaining a good stance whenever the opposition is attacking is a straightforward yet vital part of goalkeeping. The basic stance sees the legs shoulder-width apart, the arms in front, head straight and bodyweight slightly forwards. Two of the most common mistakes are too-wide stances – which make it hard to change direction – and staying flat-footed – which makes it almost impossible to move quickly. The keeper should be up on the balls of his feet whenever the ball is in a dangerous position.

▲ *To gather in a ground-level ball, get down on one knee, get your hands behind the ball and scoop it up, with your knee and foot forming a barrier.*

1

2

◄This keeper adopts the basic stance (picture second left) from which he can move to collect a ball to his right at waist height (far left) or perform a high diving save (left and below).

Communication and positioning

Goalkeeping is all about preventing attacks from becoming goals, and many attacking chances can be snuffed out using nothing more spectacular than concentration, good basic positioning and good communication. A well-placed and alert goalkeeper can often see the game in front of him better than team-mates and should relay advice to them. At set pieces such as free kicks, the keeper should be in charge of his goal area. Instructions to players should be clear, brief and calm.

▲ The above-head-height catch can be used to cut out high balls into the penalty area.

Simple saves

Many shots and loose balls can be gathered in without resorting to a dive. The secret is quick footwork and a sharp eye to get in line with the incoming ball so that your body is fully behind the ball as you collect it. Try to cushion the ball on arrival. Goalkeepers do this by taking the ball early, giving them room to bring their hands back as the ball impacts, so killing its pace. Remember: soft hands equals safe hands. Shots, loose crosses, stray passes and knockdowns come at different heights, so keepers need to practise a range of ball-taking skills at waist, chest, ground, thigh and head height.

▲ With his arms 20–30cm in front of his body, the keeper gets his hands behind and to the sides of the ball with his fingers spread out.

> **MASTERCLASS**
> Goalkeeping basics
>
> Maintain a good stance on the balls of your feet and with your head up, ready for action.
>
> ———
>
> Get your body in line with an incoming ball and always watch it right into your hands.
>
> ———
>
> If you decide to go for a ball, call loudly, and be positive, determined and decisive.

No.11 Gordon Banks

Gordon Banks was one of the finest keepers of his or any other era. Career highlights included a stunning save from Pelé in the 1970 World Cup and winning the 1966 World Cup with England.

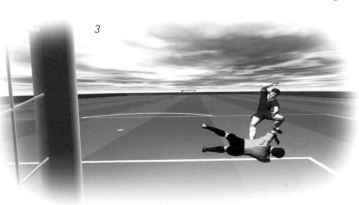

◄With the attacker clean through on goal, the keeper comes off his line to narrow the angle (1). Staying upright as long as possible (2), the keeper performs a smothering save, diving at the feet of the attacker, spreading himself and gathering in the ball (3).

3

Goalkeeping Choices

The best goalkeepers are good communicators and know how to concentrate. A goalkeeper must also make many decisions, quickly and calmly, throughout a match. A keeper has a number of different goal-stopping techniques to master, including punching the ball and diving saves. Dealing with backpasses and distributing the ball to team-mates are also essential skills.

MASTERCLASS
Goalkeeping choices

If a player in your half isn't free, kick a long ball upfield.

Good, clear communication can prevent many defensive errors.

Put any mistakes you make behind you and concentrate on the rest of the game.

Remember the three 'B's of goalkeeping – Be positive, Be the boss, Be first.

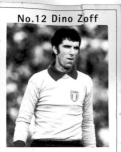

No.12 Dino Zoff

Italian goalkeeper Dino Zoff was a fine shot-stopper and very calm under pressure. He once went a record 1,143 minutes without conceding a goal. He played at international level until the age of 41.

▶ *A dramatic leap to deflect the ball is sometimes the only way of preventing a goal. When tipping the ball over or around the goal, the goalkeeper must stay alert for rebounds off the woodwork.*

Punch or deflect?
Although a two-handed catch is the ideal save to make, it's not always possible to get both hands fully on the ball. Sometimes, punching or deflecting are the only options. To punch a ball, use both fists placed close together and angled slightly inwards. With wrists firm, aim to punch just below the middle of the ball with a short but strong jabbing action. On other occasions, you'll be at full stretch and the only way of preventing a goal will be to deflect or tip the ball around the post or over the bar.

◀ *Sometimes, a goalkeeper can be too ambitious. Colombian goalkeeper René Higuita threw caution to the wind when he tried to dribble the ball past Cameroon's Roger Milla during the 1990 World Cup. Milla scored and Cameroon went on to win the game 2-1.*

◀ *Moving across the goal from the basic stance (1), this goalkeeper launches himself off one foot (2) and gets his hands behind the ball (3). He uses his body and arms to prevent the ball from spilling out as he lands (4).*

1   2   3   4

Diving

Every goalkeeper has to make diving saves. The ball should be taken in front of the body and always watched onto the hands. Gather the ball in as quickly as possible to prevent it from spilling out. One of the most difficult dives for a goalkeeper is the low drop onto the ball. To respond to a shot fired low and near to your body, push your legs away and get your body down and behind the ball.

▶ *French goalkeeper Fabien Barthez performs an underarm throw. With his front foot pointing at his target, he releases the ball and follows through smoothly.*

Distribution

You've saved the ball – what now? You have to decide whether to distribute the ball either by foot or by hand. Throws tend to be more accurate, although kicking the ball, usually using an instep volley or half-volley, can cover more distance. There are three ways of throwing the ball – the underarm roll-out, which is good for accuracy, the overarm throw for distance, and the javelin throw for which the ball is thrust forward using a bent arm. The javelin throw is often the quickest way of distributing the ball.

◀ *For an overarm throw, the arm should be kept relatively straight as it swings over with a bowling motion. A wide stance helps provide balance.*

◀ *Barthez releases the ball from his hand and connects with it on the volley using his instep. Hit hard enough and with enough height, the ball will reach players in the other half of the field.*

Backpass rule

The backpass rule was introduced to cut down on timewasting. The rule says that a throw-in or intentional pass back to the goalkeeper cannot be handled. If it is, an indirect free kick will be awarded to the other team. Don't try to be clever and attempt some fancy dribbling when the ball comes back to you. Hit a backpass cleanly and immediately or, if you have plenty of time and space, cushion and control the ball before sending it upfield. If you're under pressure, it's far better to give away a throw-in rather than a possible scoring chance.

▲ *Using his arms for balance, legendary Danish goalkeeper Peter Schmeichel hits another big goal kick with the instep of his boot.*

See also

24-25 Movement and Space |

26-27 On-ball Skills |

20-21 Passing |

22-23 Advanced Passing

▲ *As he approaches the defender, the wide player with the ball passes to his team-mate.*

▲ *With the defender caught in two minds, the wide player makes an overlapping run down the line.*

▲ *The wide player receives the return pass and now has time and space to make a cross or cut infield.*

Attacking Skills

Attacking is not just the preserve of two or three forwards. Counter attacks are often started by defenders and driven forwards by midfielders, while many crosses come from full-backs out near the sideline. Every outfield player can take part in attacking moves and so should develop the key skills involved.

Overloads and overlaps

Attacks that use plenty of a pitch's space, its width and depth, can stretch defences and lead to goalscoring chances. Giving your attack depth means staggering your positions up the pitch. This not only allows the on-ball player to make a safe pass backwards, it also makes it very difficult for a defence to mark up and play the offside trap against you. Width is very important, as defences tend to concentrate in the middle of the pitch, and an overlapping run by a wide player down the touchline can lead to a great crossing opportunity. Always be on the lookout for an 'overload'. An overload occurs when the attacking side has more players in the attacking third of the pitch than the defending side. This requires fast running and support from team-mates.

"Football should always be played beautifully; you should play in an attacking way; it must be a spectacle." Johan Cruyff

▲ *Giving your attack depth gives you more options. Here, a pass has been made to the player on the far left who is making a late run into the area, staying onside and joining the attack at the last moment.*

MASTERCLASS
Attacking skills

Always look to support an attacking team-mate with the ball, offering him passing and laying-off options.

Aim to cross the ball with accuracy as well as pace – don't just punt the ball into the area.

Split up into groups of defenders and attackers when practising attacking moves in training games and drills.

Opening up spaces

Sometimes attackers break away from a marker or find space to receive the ball. On other occasions, they move to create space for others to exploit. Attacking without the ball is very important and often involves an attacker making a quick change of direction or pace to take a defender with him. As the defender moves to cover his opponent, space that another attacker can run into appears.

▲ *A diagonal run across and into a defence, as made by the player in yellow on the left, can cause hesitancy among defenders. They may be unsure whether to follow him, opening up space for another attacker, or to leave him free.*

▶ *Most crosses have to be hit when a player is on the move, so practise crossing by running with the ball for approximately ten metres before hitting it into the penalty area.*

▲ *Bordeaux's Corentin Martins prepares to swing a cross into the penalty area. Use an instep drive to add pace to the ball.*

Crossing the ball

A cross is simply a pass from out wide into the penalty area but it can be deadly if hit with accuracy. Players work hard on their crossing and tend to use the instep-drive pass to hit the ball with pace into the target area. Aimless punts into the box are easily defended. Make sure you glance up to locate a target before you make a cross. You're looking to get the ball onto a team-mate's head or in front of them for a shot. Hitting the byline means crossing from close to the end of the pitch. A cross from this position is harder for a keeper to collect as the ball tends to be moving away from him.

No.13 Gianfranco Zola

As well as being a scorer of some classic goals, the skilful Italian also has the vision to pick out team-mates in better positions than himself with unerring accuracy.

See also

12-13 Key Rules

30-31 Volleying and Shooting

42-43 Attacking Skills

Opening up Defences

Many attacks break down as a result of slow or lazy thinking. Defensive techniques, such as offside traps, where the entire defence move up in a line to catch forwards out, prey on sloppy attacking. Quick, accurate movement and passing can open up even the sternest of defences.

▲ Blessed with blistering pace, vision and skill, the Ukrainian star Andri Shevchenko has managed to keep his goalscoring touch in the toughest defensive league in the world – Italy's Serie A, in which he plays for AC Milan.

Attacking passes and through balls

The closer you get to the opponent's goal, the less time and space there tends to be. A top-quality attacking pass should be placed and paced so that the receiver can do something with it with their first touch of the ball. Passes for attackers to run onto must be carefully weighted so that they don't speed too far ahead of the receiver and get cut out. Passes behind defenders, often known as 'through balls', take those defenders out of the game but they require expert timing and teamwork between players.

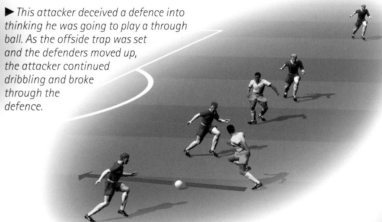

► This attacker deceived a defence into thinking he was going to play a through ball. As the offside trap was set and the defenders moved up, the attacker continued dribbling and broke through the defence.

▲ The attacker on the left drags a defender out of position, just enough for a through ball to be played between the two defenders. The attacker on the right times his run to stay onside and collects the ball behind the defence.

Swerving passes

Swerving or bending the ball through the air is a technique often used in the taking of free kicks, but that is not its only value. During attacking moves, the ability to swerve the ball can be very useful. Swerving the ball (see page 57) involves kicking through one side of it with a long follow-through. This action puts sidespin on the ball which sends it off on a curved path. Inswinging and outswinging passes can clear opponents to find a team-mate in a good position. Swerved shots can get around a defence and outfox the opposition keeper.

Scoring goals

A good attacking move doesn't guarantee a goal. For that you need clinical finishing from whoever receives the ball in a goalscoring position. The role of other attackers at this point is far from over. In fact, following up a goalbound header or shot is vital, as many goals at all levels come from rebounds off players or the goal. Good awareness is a vital quality in a forward as he or she must quickly judge which team-mate is in the best position to try to score.

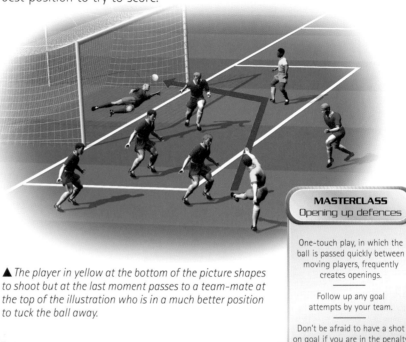

No.14 Emilio Butragueño

The winner of five league titles in a row with Real Madrid, Spanish striker Butragueño was nicknamed the vulture for his lightning reactions and awareness in the penalty area.

▲ *The on-ball player has a choice. He can cross the ball to the player on the right-hand side of the area using an outswinging swerved pass. Or he can simply send a short, straight pass to another free team-mate.*

▲ *The player in yellow at the bottom of the picture shapes to shoot but at the last moment passes to a team-mate at the top of the illustration who is in a much better position to tuck the ball away.*

▼ *Aston Villa forward Julian Joachim (centre) threads a ball past the outstretched foot of Leicester City's Matt Elliott for strike partner Stan Collymore (right) to run onto.*

MASTERCLASS
Opening up defences

One-touch play, in which the ball is passed quickly between moving players, frequently creates openings.

Follow up any goal attempts by your team.

Don't be afraid to have a shot on goal if you are in the penalty area and no real alternative options are on offer.

See also

28–29 Tackling

48–49 Defending as a Unit

62–63 Formations

Defending

"Strikers win you games but defenders win you championships."

John Gregory

When the opposition has the ball, it's time to defend. Defending is sometimes seen as the least glamorous side of the game but a goal prevented by a watchful, expert defence is just as valuable as a spectacular strike by your side. Skilled defenders are prized assets at all clubs.

Regaining possession

Defending has two prime aims – to stop the opposition scoring and to regain possession of the ball. Regaining the ball can sometimes involve tackling but there are other ways such as jockeying and delaying an opponent and pressurizing him into making a mistake. One vitally important method is closing down space. This means you and your team-mates getting into goalside positions, working together to cut out space for opposition attacks and tracking attackers who run into dangerous positions.

▲ *Arsenal's Sylvain Wiltord is challenged by Queen's Park Rangers' Clarke Carlisle. Tackling is a vital part of defending but isn't the only way to regain possession.*

Jockeying

Getting in the way of an attacker with the ball is a vital part of defending known as 'jockeying'. When an opposition player with the ball approaches, close in on him. Don't close in too much – or he may find it easy to go round you – but enough to cut out space in front of him. Get into a defensive stance with your body weight over your knees, standing on the balls of your feet, with your arms out for balance. Move with the player, keeping at a similar distance and staying goalside of him. By holding up the attacker, you are buying time for team-mates to get back into stronger defensive positions.

◄ *German striker Jürgen Klinsmann tries to jockey Pavel Pardo of Mexico, proving that defenders are not the only ones who use defensive skills.*

Forcing a weaker position

Apart from delaying a player, jockeying is about forcing the attacker into a weaker position while staying goalside of him. One option is to try to guide him out towards a sideline – a less threatening position, where he will have relatively little space and few options.

▲ Pressure from Bayern Munich forces Real Madrid's Jose Mari Gutierrez to make a mistake and lose track of the ball.

▲ Wolverhampton Wanderers' George Ndah jockeys Mark Patterson of Gillingham away from goal.

From this position, it may be easier to challenge him. If your opponent has his back to goal when receiving the ball, you are in a strong jockeying position, and your main task is to prevent the player turning to face the goal without giving away a foul. Done well, jockeying may force a mistake or, at least, a pass back and away from your goal. Stick with the attacker if he attempts to turn and run into space behind you.

◀ Albania's Geri Cipi takes the full force of Michael Owen's powerful shot.

▲ The defender in blue clears while under pressure from the attacker in yellow.

No.15 Bobby Moore

The captain of England's 1966 World-Cup-winning side was a superb tackler and a great reader of the game. Pelé described him as, "the best defender I ever played against".

Get rid of it!

Great defenders such as Germany's Franz Beckenbauer were excellent at playing the ball skilfully out of defence before hitting an accurate pass to a team-mate to set up an attacking move. However, even the very best defenders know that if the ball comes to them when under pressure, they should think safety first when making a clearance. This can mean safe passing into space or, when under severe pressure, getting plenty of height and distance on the ball to take it well away from the danger zone and your goal.

See also

14-15 Fouls and Misconduct

28-29 Tackling

32-33 Heading

▼ French defender Marcel Desailly clears the ball while under pressure from Australian Mark Viduka.

Defending as a Unit

Preventing an opposition attack leading to a goal is key to defending and the reason why teams defend as a unit. Attackers shouldn't let the back four or five players and the goalkeeper do the work. Defending is the responsibility of all 11 players. There are different roles for different player positions, but many of the basic rules of defending apply to all.

Defending from the front

Intelligent, committed defending begins at the front line and goes all the way back. The attackers' role in defence is an important one. They are the front line of defence, looking to restrict the opposition's space, chase down passes between opponents and harass these players into making mistakes. Good defensive work by attackers can put the opposition player on the ball under pressure. This can result in him making an aimless punt forward for your side to collect, or even an interception and immediate attacking chance.

MASTERCLASS
Defending as a unit

Don't dive in to intercept the ball or make a challenge until you have cover behind you.

Communication is vital when defending, especially at set pieces such as corners or free kicks.

Don't get distracted when marking – keep positioned to watch your opponent first and the game second.

Interception

Stealing the ball from the opposition as it travels from passer to receiver can be a clean, efficient way of regaining possession. It can also leave you in space to move away quickly and start an attack. Intercepting a ball simply requires speed off the mark, and calls for quickness of thought, awareness of where players are, and judgement of the ball's pace and direction. In short, you need to decide whether you can get to the ball before the opposition. A failed interception leaves the ball with your opponents and you out of position and out of the game.

▲ The blue midfielder has spotted an underhit pass and is about to make an interception. The further from goal you are, the less risky this move becomes.

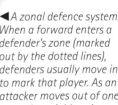

◀ A zonal defence system. When a forward enters a defender's zone (marked out by the dotted lines), defenders usually move in to mark that player. As an attacker moves out of one zone, the neighbouring defender can pick him up.

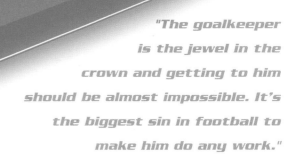

▶ A player-to-player marking system used in your side's defensive third of the pitch relies on additional players to act as spare defenders, putting the attacker on the ball under pressure.

No.16 Paolo Maldini

Capable of spotting danger from a distance, Maldini has played as a sweeper, left-back and in the centre of defence for AC Milan and Italy, and was one of the finest players of the 1990s.

▼ Marking is about getting relatively close to an opposition forward and not giving him the time or space to receive the ball. Try to stay goalside of your opponent and in a position to see the game developing in front of you.

"The goalkeeper is the jewel in the crown and getting to him should be almost impossible. It's the biggest sin in football to make him do any work."

George Graham

Defensive systems

There are two main ways in which a team works defensively as a unit. The first is by marking up player-to-player, for which defenders mark one player and stick with him whenever the opposition is on the attack. The second system is zonal defence, where players are responsible for certain areas or zones of the pitch that all overlap, providing some cover. These zones can move up and down the pitch as the play dictates. Teams often mix systems, for example, playing a largely zonal defence but giving one defender the task of player-marking a particularly dangerous attacker.

▼ Vaclav Budka of Czech side FK Jablonec positions himself by the post ready to defend a corner and make a goal-line clearance if necessary.

▼ Marking up at set pieces such as corners is essential. The blue team have used their central defenders to mark the tallest attackers. Other players are positioned by the posts and the edge of the area.

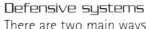
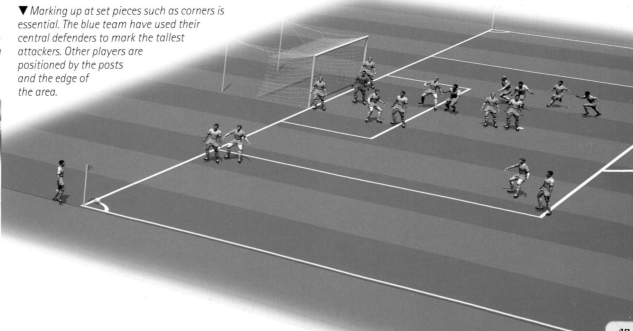

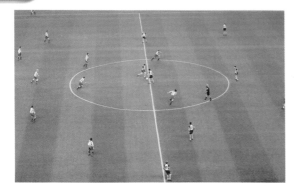

▲ *A kick-off opens a game between Atletico Madrid and Borussia Dortmund during a 1996 UEFA Champions League encounter. The player who kicks off is not allowed to have the second touch of the ball.*

Restarts

Play can be stopped during a game for a number of reasons. These include when the ball leaves the pitch, a goal is scored or a foul is committed. The way play is resumed depends on the kind of stoppage. For example, when the ball crosses a sideline, the officials will signal a throw-in. Corners, goal kicks, free-kicks, kick-offs and drop balls are other types of restarts.

The kick-off

Every game begins with a kick-off. This set piece is also played whenever a goal is scored and at the start of the second half. The ball has to be moved forwards over the halfway line by the kicking-off team, while the opposition must stay in their half – but not enter the centre circle – until the ball has been kicked. Many teams play the ball back after it has been tapped forwards. Others launch a wide pass out to a flank hoping that a winger can collect the ball and immediately attack the opposition's goalmouth.

◄ *Your hands should be spread around the back of the ball so that your thumbs almost touch. Too far around the sides and the ball can become harder to control.*

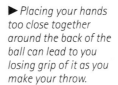

▶ *Placing your hands too close together around the back of the ball can lead to you losing grip of it as you make your throw.*

◄ *With feet firmly planted on the ground and ball behind your head, arch your back and thrust your upper body and arms forwards. Release the ball just before your arms come over your head.*

▲ *This is a foul throw on three different counts – the front foot is completely over the sideline, the trailing foot is off the ground and only one hand is on the ball when the player makes the throw-in.*

Throw-ins

Throw-ins have to be taken from close to where the ball crossed the sideline. Officials usually penalize players who persistently try to gain extra ground before making the throw. Players of all standards are often penalized for foul throws. There are a few key rules you need to remember – your feet need to be behind the sideline, the ball brought back behind your head, and both hands must be on the ball. Both feet must be touching the ground as the throw is made and the ball is released. If you commit a foul throw, the opposing team is awarded the throw-in.

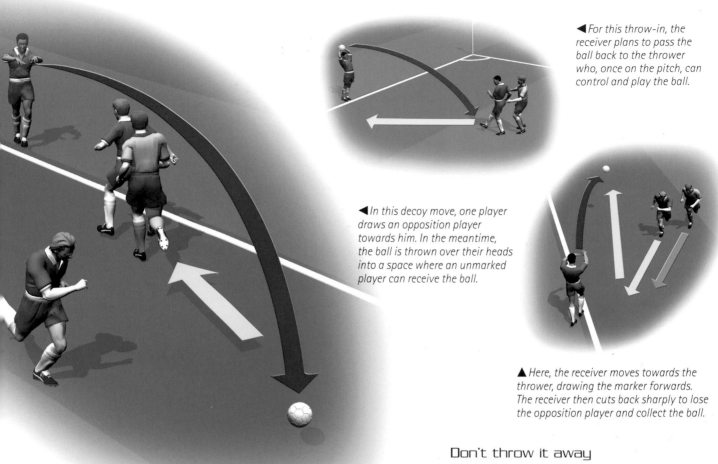

◄ For this throw-in, the receiver plans to pass the ball back to the thrower who, once on the pitch, can control and play the ball.

◄ In this decoy move, one player draws an opposition player towards him. In the meantime, the ball is thrown over their heads into a space where an unmarked player can receive the ball.

▲ Here, the receiver moves towards the thrower, drawing the marker forwards. The receiver then cuts back sharply to lose the opposition player and collect the ball.

Longer throws

Long throws can get a ball directly into an opponent's penalty area. Even if you can't propel the ball that far, longer throws give you potentially more team-mates to aim for and can be helpful for clearing the ball upfield. Take several quick steps up to the sideline and pull the ball right back behind your head. Arch your back as much as possible, then uncoil your back and arms to catapult the ball forwards. Keep most of your weight on the front leg and follow through with your hands and fingers to direct the ball.

Don't throw it away

Treat throw-ins like you would any other set piece and practise a range of different throw-in moves. Avoid giving the ball away cheaply with a foul throw or a half-hearted throw that can be easily intercepted by the other side. Try to throw to a team-mate who is unmarked and at a height that allows him to control the ball quickly and easily. Aim to throw to your team-mate's feet, thigh or head for a flick-on to another member of your side. A ball that bounces waist-high in front of a player can be extremely difficult to control.

◄ Tranmere Rovers' Dave Challinor holds the world record for the longest throw-in, with a distance of 46.34m. It came, according to Challinor, 'after 29 dreadful attempts.'

▲ A drop ball is given by a referee when there has been a temporary break in play, such as when a player has been accidentally injured. One player from each side contests the ball, which can only be kicked when it has hit the ground.

See also

32–33 Heading

44–45 Opening up Defences

48–49 Defending as a Unit

The Corner Kick

When a ball runs over a team's goal line and was last touched by a player from that team, the referee signals a corner. A corner is a dangerous situation for the defending team and a great opportunity for the attacking side.

Corner advantages

Corners are similar to crosses in open play but with some big advantages – the ball isn't moving and you choose when to hit it. There are other pluses – defenders have to be at least nine metres away from the ball, you can have plenty of team-mates in the penalty area as targets to aim for, and the offside rule doesn't apply. But there's also one disadvantage – defenders will be closely marking your side's players.

◀ *Teams practise different corner kicks in training. Here, the player signals to his team-mates which type of corner to expect.*

The art of a good corner

Good corners are hit with pace and accuracy – they should arrive in the target area a little above head height. Slow, high, looping corners are easily cleared by defenders. When you take a corner, you should feel completely balanced on your non-kicking foot and strike through the middle or just below the middle of the ball. The kicking leg follows through and across the body as the body turns into the cross.

No.17 Luis Figo

The Portuguese striker Luis Figo is known for the accuracy and power of his corner kicks. In 2000, he was bought by Real Madrid for what was then a record fee of £39 million.

▲ *For a corner from the left-hand side of the pitch (from the attacking team's viewpoint), this is where you should place the ball if you're right-footed.*

Aiming long

Most corners are taken long and hit with enough power to reach the six-yard box or even closer to the goal. The classic target area is a point just in front of the near or far post. Inswinging corners swerve towards the goal, outswinging ones away from the goal. Both can be lethal.

◀ *This is where you should place the ball if you're left-footed. Using the left foot from this position can create an outswinging corner.*

▶ *An inswinging corner usually bends into the six-yard box. Some inswinging corners have enough power and bend to hit the back of the net without a touch from another player.*

◀ *Near-post corners allow a flick-on header by a team-mate (yellow arrows). Deeper corners to the far post can give a team-mate a chance of a strike behind the keeper (red arrows).*

Pace and accuracy

Another advantage of a corner hit with pace is that it is harder for defenders to clear, and a mistake or deflection can easily lead to an own goal. When a corner is driven hard, team-mates in the area may only need a touch rather than a power header or fully-fledged shot to redirect the ball over the line.

▼ ▲ *David Beckham's corners led to many goals for Manchester United. Few were more important than Ole Gunnar Solskjaer's dramatic winner against Bayern Munich in the 1999 Champions League final (above).*

MASTERCLASS
The corner kick

Aim for a target just above head height.

Strike the ball hard enough to carry it into the six-yard box.

Make sure you're completely balanced on your non-kicking foot.

Surprise your opponents with the occasional short corner.

Short corners

Taken quickly, short corners to a team-mate a few metres away can allow the cross to come in from a different angle. They can catch the defending side off-guard, with unmarked players in the box. But taken sloppily or slowly, they just waste a golden opportunity, leaving you or your team-mate stranded in the corner.

Free Kicks

If a team commits an offence, they can expect the referee to blow his whistle and award a free kick to the other side. A free kick sees the ball placed on the ground at the point where the offence was committed, while the opposing team is forced to retreat at least ten yards (nine metres). Not every free kick offers an attacking chance but all give a side valuable possession in time and in space.

▲ One exception to the ten-yards rule occurs when a team is awarded an indirect free kick inside the opponent's penalty area. The defenders are allowed to stand on their goal line even if it isn't ten yards away from the free kick.

▲ Direct or indirect, a quickly taken free kick in the middle of the pitch can open up large amounts of space and lead to attacking chances. Here, Raul of Real Madrid is showing the key trait of a quick free-kick taker, keeping his head up to view the options around him, before kicking the ball.

◀ Brazilian star Sissi is a renowned free-kick taker in the women's game.

◀ Referee Graham Barber signals that an indirect free kick has been awarded. His arm will remain in the air until the kick is taken and has either touched another player or gone out of play.

Turn defence into attack

Wherever you are on the pitch, a free kick gives you the great gift of possession – so don't waste it. Quick free kicks can open up attacking opportunities but only if you and the receiver are alert, the free kick is hit accurately and no opponent can intercept it. When awarded a free kick deep in your own half, aim to get the ball out of your danger zone and move possession upfield. Don't put your side in trouble by hitting a lazy ball or playing the ball to a team-mate who's not looking for the pass. Be aware and look around for a free player.

Indirect free kicks

An indirect free kick is so called because you cannot score directly from it – instead, the ball must be played by one other team-mate before a goal attempt can be made. Indirect free kicks are given for less-serious offences in football, including charging or obstructing a player who isn't on the ball or receiving the ball in an offside position. Goalkeepers can incur indirect free kicks if, for instance, they hold onto the ball for more than the allowed six seconds or handle a deliberate backpass.

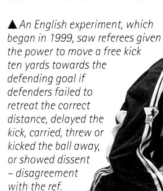

▲ *An English experiment, which began in 1999, saw referees given the power to move a free kick ten yards towards the defending goal if defenders failed to retreat the correct distance, delayed the kick, carried, threw or kicked the ball away, or showed dissent – disagreement with the ref.*

MASTERCLASS
Free kicks

Rehearse your free kicks as a team hard and often. Split up into defenders and attackers to create as realistic a situation as possible.

Keep your free-kick moves simple and effective. A move that requires more than three touches exposes it to more possibilities to break down.

Vary free kicks during a game to keep opponents guessing.

▲ *The arrows show some of the options possible from this direct free kick – bending the ball around one side of the wall of defenders, a shot up and over the wall, or rolling the ball out to the side for a team-mate to strike.*

Direct free kicks

For the more serious offences, including pushing and tripping, or a goalkeeper handling outside of his area, teams get a direct free kick. This is where the first touch can, but doesn't have to be, a direct shot on goal. Direct free kicks in central positions in the attacking third of the pitch can offer many options and are a real menace to defend against, even with a wall in place. Players and teams practise their free-kick moves long and hard to try to turn the threat into goalscoring reality.

▶ *Peruvian star Nolberto Solano, shown here playing for Newcastle United, has his head over the ball and his body well-balanced – the perfect stance from which to deliver a deadly free kick.*

▲ *Communication between the keeper and his defensive wall is vital. Here, Borussia Dortmund's Stephane Chapuisat (left) and Paulo Sousa (right) check for instructions.*

▲ *For long-range or wide free kicks, a two- or three-man wall is frequently used. When the free kick is central and close to goal, teams build a five- or six-man wall.*

Free Kicks in Attack

Free kicks give you one touch of the ball without being challenged and with the opposition some distance away. In an attacking position, this is a priceless commodity. Many games are decided on the results of free kicks, so the attacking side needs to take advantage and defenders must be alert and vigilant.

Defending a free kick

As soon as the ref gives a free kick to the opposition, get back into a defensive position. Stay alert for a quickly taken free kick – if it doesn't come, get organized, and listen to team-mates' instructions. It's vital to get men behind the ball, covering the spaces where a goalscoring chance might be created. If the free kick is likely to be a cross, taller defenders should mark good headers of the ball while other defenders look to cut out knock-downs and pick up attackers making late runs into the box.

▲ *A sidefoot pass can change the angle of attack and give the receiver the chance of a shot without the defensive wall blocking his way.*

Surprise and disguise

Some element of cunning and surprise is often required for free kicks to be successful. Don't let it be obvious what you plan to do to the opposing side – it'll make the free kick easy to defend. Dummy and decoy runs by players can cause confusion and mask the planned free-kick attempt. Attackers can form a wall in front of the real wall to hide the ball. One ploy is for several attackers to join the end of a defensive wall. This can block a goalkeeper's view, and by peeling off just before the kick is taken, can create a sudden gap for the shot to travel through.

Bending the ball

A useful skill to have on the pitch during open play, the ability to bend or swerve the ball accurately can be deadly at free kicks. Expert free-kick takers such as David Beckham, Roberto Carlos and Jay Jay Okocha all have this skill. It's a complicated technique that requires much practice and perseverance, and some players find they're better at hitting inside swerves or outside swerves. Both types of swerve involve hitting the ball low through one side and finishing with a long, relaxed follow-through.

▲ To hit an inside swerve (left), strike the ball with the inside of your boot, using a straight follow-through. For an outside swerve (right), use the outside of your boot – the follow-through should take your foot across your body.

Fast or wide

The quickly taken free kick isn't only used in the middle of the pitch to put the ball into space. A rapid move, such as a snapshot from a direct free kick, can catch a goalkeeper and his defence off-guard – just ask the England team about Dietmar Hamann's speedy strike, which won a 2002 World Cup qualifier for Germany. Wide free kicks can also offer more options than just a simple, immediate cross. An overlap down the wing can send in a cross from a more threatening angle, and a ball infield to a late-arriving runner can offer a shooting chance.

▼ The options from this position include bending the ball in for a cross, passing the ball infield or playing it down the wing for a wide player to cross from the goal line.

▶ Players on the attacking side peel off from the defensive wall causing confusion among their opponents as the free-kick taker tries a shot on goal.

▲ All successful sides, from local or school teams right up to Holland's Euro 2000 national side pictured here, practise their free-kick moves on the training ground.

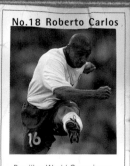

No.18 Roberto Carlos

Brazilian World Cup winner, Roberto Carlos is perhaps best known for scoring a stunning, swerving and dipping free kick from more than 25m out, against France in 1997.

See also

12-13 Key Rules

14-15 Fouls and Misconduct

30-31 Volleying and Shooting

Penalty!

A penalty kick is a free shot on goal taken from the penalty spot. Any foul that would normally see a direct free kick awarded becomes a penalty if the foul was committed inside the box. To give a penalty, referees have to judge where the foul was committed – not where the fouled player ends up. For the attacking side, a penalty is a likely goal in the making.

▲ When a penalty is given, only the referee, goalkeeper and penalty taker are allowed in the penalty area until the penalty taker has made contact with the ball. A referee can order a penalty to be retaken if any other players from either team enter the area.

▲ The penalty taker starts his run-up, noting the keeper's position. Most penalty takers have decided what sort of penalty they intend before they move towards the ball.

▲ This player has approached the ball as if he is going to put it towards the right side of the goal as he views it. The keeper commits early and starts to move in that direction.

▲ The penalty taker wraps his foot around the ball and uses a firm, low sidefoot pass to place the ball into the opposite corner of the goal.

The mental game

Zico, Platini, Baggio – these and dozens more star players have all missed penalty kicks in crucial situations. So how do high-calibre players miss such a clear chance on goal? In a single word, pressure. In a few more words, pressure and plenty of time for a player's thoughts to get the better of him. The good news is that, at all levels of football, if you can keep your nerve, the task in front of you is relatively simple. You're just 11m away from goal and have only the keeper on his line to beat. The odds are certainly stacked in the penalty taker's favour.

Chip, blast or place

For professional players, the choice of penalty shot is great. Some players prefer the cheeky chip over an early diving keeper into the back of the middle of the net. Many choose to blast the ball as hard as possible or aim a driven shot into a corner. Throw in the possibility of feints and dummies during the run-up, and the preparation of dossiers on rivals' penalty takers and goalkeepers, and it soon becomes a confusing array of options. The placed penalty is the most popular choice for non-professional footballers. This is a relatively simple shot made with the side of the foot, hitting the ball firmly but under control into one of the goal's four corners.

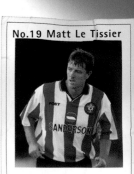

No.19 Matt Le Tissier

Matt Le Tissier retired in 2002, but he will always remain a legend at Southampton, in part due to his success with penalty kicks. In 1999-2000 he scored 48 penalties from 49 attempts.

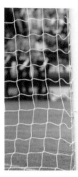

▲ *The 2001 Champions League final saw Bayern Munich's Oliver Kahn (above) and Valencia's Santiago Canizares save penalties in the shootout. Bayern ended up winners.*

The keeper's view

As a keeper facing either a normal penalty or a penalty shootout, you should be calm and relaxed. A goal from a penalty is expected but if the opposition push or blast the penalty high or wide, you'll be delighted, but if you actually save their attempt, then you'll be a 24-carat hero. It is very much up to you as a keeper what you do at a penalty. Keepers are allowed to move along their line, but not off it, before the penalty is taken. Some keepers, just like penalty takers, decide in advance which way to go and dive at full-stretch as the kick is taken, or choose instead to remain upright. Others try to read the taker's intentions or, if they've come up against the taker before, try to recall the most likely direction.

▼ *Practise penalties using a goal and two cones, each placed one metre in from the goalposts. Aim to send your kicks between the cones and the goalposts.*

MASTERCLASS
Penalty!

Decide early where you intend putting the penalty and don't change your mind in the run-up.

Keep your head down and your body balanced as you take the kick.

Stay alert and aware after taking a regular penalty for a second chance following a save. Other players should follow up after the kick has been taken to both attack and defend.

▲ *The goalkeeper as heroine – USA keeper Briana Scurry made the save that saw the US win a tense shootout with China, 5-4, and collect the 1999 World Cup.*

▼ *Paraguay goalkeeper Jose Luis Chilavert is famous both for taking free kicks and penalties and for saving them.*

▲ *Italian Roberto Baggio blazed his 1994 World Cup final penalty over the crossbar, handing the trophy to Brazil. Baggio did, however, score two spot kicks at the 1998 World Cup.*

Penalty shootouts

Many knockout competitions use penalty shootouts to decide the outcome of a game when the scores are still level after extra-time. A shootout usually calls for five players on each side to take alternate penalties and if the score is level after those ten kicks, more players, one from each side, continue until there is a winner. Although labelled as cruel on individuals, penalty shootouts are pure theatre and, many believe, a fairer way of deciding the outcome than drawing lots or flipping a coin.

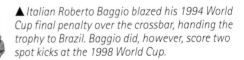

▲ *Stuart Pearce made up for a miss at the 1990 World Cup with a successful spot kick in the Euro 96 shootout with Spain. The image of him celebrating is an enduring memory of the tournament.*

▲ Real Madrid manager Vicente Del Bosque (far right), stands in front of his team's substitutes' bench watching the game intensely.

> *"You must believe you are the best and then make sure that you are."*
>
> **Bill Shankly**

▶ A passion for the game and the ability to motivate players are hallmarks of successful managers such as Liverpool legend Bill Shankly, who transformed his club.

Managers and Coaches

No one feels the pressures of football more than the person in charge of shaping the team, selecting which players will play and in what positions, and choosing which tactics. At some clubs, this responsibility is split between a director of football, who oversees the club's development and is involved with transfers, and a first-team manager or coach, who works with the players. At other clubs, it's all down to one individual, usually known as the manager.

◀ Many ex-pros move into management. Others, such as Paul Power, head of Manchester City's youth development, are employed behind the scenes to work with a club's younger players.

Head of a team

Although they usually receive most of the attention, modern-day managers and coaches tend to be part of a large team of backroom staff. They frequently employ a second-in-command, an assistant coach who helps with the day-to-day running of the first-team squad. There are often additional coaches in charge of the youth and reserve teams as well as scouts who scour regions, countries and even continents on the lookout for fresh footballing talent. Fitness trainers, physiotherapists and other medical staff, kit men, and sometimes sports psychologists who help to focus the players mentally, complete what is a good-sized team, all working behind the scenes at a club.

▲ In some countries, club managers and coaches assist with the national set-up. Here, Peter Taylor and Steve McClaren are working with the England national team.

Pressure cooker

Despite being part of a team, the manager or coach of a club can often find himself under immense pressure, particularly at the top sides for which success is expected. Managers' reputations stand or fall on their player selections, their transfer wheelings and dealings, and by the tactical decisions they make in individual games or over a campaign. But above all, managers are judged on their team's results. It can take only a handful of disappointing scorelines for managers to be criticized in the media, and by supporters and owners. Continued failings inevitably lead to speculation over their future employment. In the past, many managers spent decades at the same club. Today, with the financial stakes much higher and the pressure to deliver trophies far greater, the managerial merry-go-round sees managers in and out of work with alarming rapidity.

▲ Arsenal's chairman David Dein raises the AXA FA cup whilst manager Arsene Wenger parades the Barclaycard Premiership trophy for the fans after Arsenal wins the Double in 2002.

▲ Club officials at Real Madrid welcome Zinedine Zidane in 2001 after he was signed for a world record fee of over £45 million.

◀ Argentina coach Cesar Luis Menotti controversially left Diego Maradona out of his 1978 World-Cup-winning squad.

A manager's duties

An excellent footballing brain, top-notch people and decision-making skills, and a vision of how the team will develop and should play, are vital requirements for the modern manager or coach. A manager's tasks include structuring the players' coaching and training, dealing with the media, working on specific skills, playing styles and set pieces, and checking out upcoming opponents and possible transfer targets. In addition, a manager has to assess the form and ability of new players, youngsters and footballers returning from injury, deciding when to play them and in what position.

▲ Some well-known managers together including, on the back row, Arsène Wenger, Sir Alex Ferguson, Fabio Capello, Rinus Michels and Gérard Houllier, and on the front row, Dr Jozef Venglos, Andy Roxburgh and Roy Hodgson.

◀ Manager Ottmar Hitzfeld celebrates with his triumphant Bayern Munich team, moments after they collected the 2001 Champions League trophy.

Club and country

With football clubs becoming increasingly big business, a manager's ability to wheel and deal profitably in the transfer market is considered a major asset. Some managers have earned themselves excellent reputations for their uncanny knack of buying players cheaply and selling them on at a later date for a much higher fee. An astute transfer swoop can invigorate and inspire a club and bring them honours. Replacing valued players with underperforming ones, on the other hand, often leads to the sack. International managers don't have the pleasure of dealing with transfers, but instead they must endure the major headache of selecting a successful team from a much wider base of players. They must also be able to cope with the phenomenal pressure and the expectations of an entire nation. Be it club or country, all managers fear failure, and dream of the glory and satisfaction that comes with success.

Formations

All football teams need a structure with players organized into a basic shape called a formation. Formations tend to be described in terms of the numbers of outfield players from the defence forwards, so 4-4-2 describes a system of four defenders, four midfielders and finally, two attackers. The following are some of the most important formations and systems in football history.

"Football is self-expression within an organized framework."
Roger Lemerre, French national coach

Major William Suddell
of Preston North End

2-3-5
Preston North End coach Major William Suddell was just one of many managers to adopt the first commonly used formation, 2-3-5. It featured five forwards with three midfielders, known as half-backs, and just one pair of full-backs defending the goal. The key player was the centre-half who played in the middle of the pitch and was the main playmaker in attack but also had to get back to mark the opposition team's centre-forward. While sides in Europe and South America tinkered with a variety of different formations, most teams in Britain stuck with 2-3-5 until the mid-1920s.

W-M (3-2-2-3)
Changes to the offside law for the 1925-26 season initially saw teams struggle to contain a five-man attack. After a 7-0 defeat to Newcastle, Arsenal manager Herbert Chapman decided to pull his centre-half back into defence and move two of his forwards back into midfield. Arsenal beat West Ham 4-0 with this new W-M formation two days later. It was called 'W-M' because the forwards formed a 'W' shape and the defenders an 'M' shape. Many other sides adopted this system and, for a quarter of a century, it was used all over the world.

Arsenal manager
Herbert Chapman

4-2-4
Brazil, under the management of Vicente Feola, arrived at the 1958 World Cup finals with two secret weapons – a 17-year-old attacker we now know as Pelé, and a system designed to counter the old W-M formation. The 4-2-4 system saw a strong defensive line of four players, with two midfielders controlling and directing play for a pair of wingers and two central strikers. Although this formation proved successful for Brazil and some other sides, it is rarely used in the modern game as it places too much emphasis on the midfield players, who may be outnumbered.

Vicente Feola

Catenaccio (1-4-3-2)

Italian for 'big chain', *catenaccio* means creating a defensively strong side, often at the expense of the attack. Central to this formation is the role of the sweeper, who plays behind the defence, mopping up loose balls and covering challenges. Under Helenio Herrera, coach of the highly successful Inter Milan team of the 1960s, *catenaccio* frequently stifled opposition attacks. Teams playing this system often relied on fast breaks by small numbers of attackers to score.

Helenio Herrera, coach of Inter Milan

4-3-3

From the 1960s onwards, football tactics became increasingly defensive. Even the most attack-minded of international sides, such as Brazil, withdrew one of their forwards back into midfield to play with a 4-3-3 formation. Brazil won the World Cup in 1962 and 1970 with this system. 4-3-3 is still used to this day – often, ironically, as an attacking alternative for a team that's behind, with time running out. One of the forwards, usually with excellent dribbling and crossing skills, takes up a wide position in attack and may switch from side to side, searching for openings.

Aymore Moriera led Brazil to glory in 1962

4-4-2

4-4-2 dispenses with wingers in favour of a four-man midfield. One of the first to use it was England manager Sir Alf Ramsey, whose 'wingless wonders' lifted the 1966 World Cup, despite initial criticism of their playing style. Its strengths are that it provides two waves of four players to defend and close down the opposition. Its weakness is that the two strikers need to cover a lot of ground and must receive support from the midfielders to launch meaningful attacks. It is one of the most commonly used formations in the modern game.

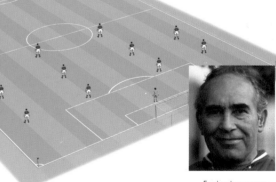

England manager Sir Alf Ramsey

3-2-3-2

Inspired by Dutch coach Rinus Michels, 'total football' saw a team's players interchange positions and roles fluidly, a system that required every player to be comfortable on the ball. It is rare to see total football today. More common are 4-4-2 and the 3-2-3-2, or wing-back, formations. The two key features of this latter formation are the three centre-backs, one of whom may be asked to man-to-man mark an opposing striker, and the two wide players – the wing-backs. Wing-backs have to cover the entire flank of a pitch, linking up in midfield and attack, as well as defending.

Rinus Michels

Tactics

Within the chosen basic formation, a manager or coach has plenty of room to try out different tactics, systems and ploys. Over the last 50 years, there have been a great number of innovations in tactical thinking that have seen subtle alterations to certain formations. There has also been a development of moves and tactics within these formations.

▶ *Sweepers such as Italy's Gaetano Scirea (left) can play defensively – rarely straying ahead of fellow defenders – or can move up to attack.*

▲ *An Argentina defender challenges Dutchman Johan Neeskens. Modern wing-backs need to get forward, as well as performing defensive duties.*

Options and systems

There are many variations and options within each formation. For example, sweepers can be used defensively or as a potential attacking weapon (see illustration top left). The same is the case for a system featuring wing-backs (left). Wing-backs can be instructed to stay back, creating a five-man defence. Alternatively, they can shuttle back and forth, helping out in defence and attack, or they can surge forwards, becoming wingers and creating an overload up front.

Another option, in midfield and attack, is called the diamond system. This involves four midfielders, or three midfielders and a striker, forming a diamond shape on the pitch. At the head of the diamond, furthest upfield, is an attacking midfielder or striker who makes late runs into position and links the midfield with the attack. Because the diamond system creates a great deal of depth up front, it can be hard for teams to defend.

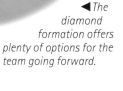

◀ *The diamond formation offers plenty of options for the team going forward.*

In the hole

Many sides play a pair of attackers or just a lone striker in the most forward position, with another player positioned behind the front line. This footballer plays in what is called 'the hole' and can be a massive threat to the opposition. He stays onside and can prompt attacks by precise passing and through balls or, if defenders back off, he can advance and unleash a long-range shot.

◀ *Juventus' Didier Deschamps (centre) shields the ball from Marc Overmars of Ajax. Deschamps often played as a midfield 'anchor', sitting in front of the defence and breaking up attacks.*

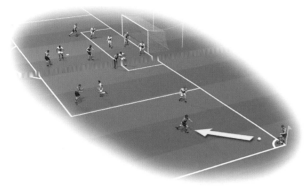

▲ There is always a risk involved in playing the offside trap and that applies even when an attack develops from a short corner, as is the case in the above illustration.

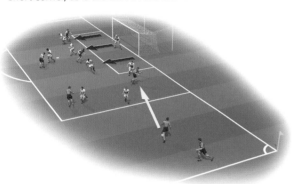

▲ The attacker shapes to pass to a team-mate (yellow arrow). Most of the defence has moved upfield but the defender marking the likely receiver keeps him onside.

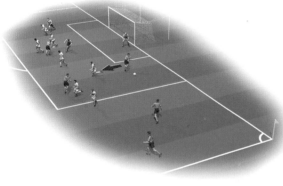

▲ The defender must step up before the ball is played to force the attacker offside. If the defender is not quick enough, the attacker would have a good chance to score.

▼ Norway use the long throw to get the ball quickly into Yugoslavia's penalty area during a Euro 2000 qualifier.

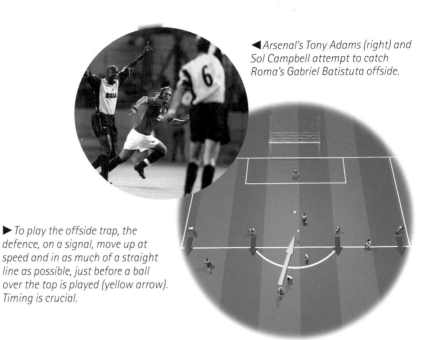

◄ Arsenal's Tony Adams (right) and Sol Campbell attempt to catch Roma's Gabriel Batistuta offside.

► To play the offside trap, the defence, on a signal, move up at speed and in as much of a straight line as possible, just before a ball over the top is played (yellow arrow). Timing is crucial.

The offside trap

When an attacker is offside, possession passes to the defending team so many sides adopt a defensive tactic, known as the offside trap, to make this happen as often as possible. The offside trap involves the back three or four players maintaining a straight line across the pitch as they suddenly move upfield to catch an opponent offside. Performed well, the offside trap can be infuriating for the opposition but it does carry the risk of being sprung, leaving no defensive cover during an attack.

► Long-ball teams often use a target man. Here, John Fashanu (left) plays that role.

The long-ball game

Some teams prefer to build attacks patiently with the emphasis on keeping possession and switching the direction of play to probe an opposition defence for an opening. A contrasting tactic is rapid and direct. A long-ball pass out of defence or midfield to an advanced attacker can quickly open up a game. The role of this target player is to get to the ball first and then control it. From there, he may either turn and attack the goal himself or hold onto the ball long enough to release a team-mate who has arrived in support. For a defender, it is possible to largely bypass the midfield and send long balls up to the strikers.

Tactics in a Game

▲ A fourth official holds up his electronic board to indicate a substitution.

Once the game starts, managers have to hope that their formation, tactics and player selection all conspire to give their side victory. But it doesn't always work out that way. Opposition teams can spring tactical surprises, and decisions and luck can go against a team, and certain players can be found wanting. In order to react to such events, managers can make extra changes to their side's tactics and play throughout the entire game.

Assessing the game

From kick-off onwards, managers and their coaching staff study the action, checking out the opposition's tactics and looking for weaknesses or mismatches on either side. For the players involved in the game, it can be hard to assess how things are going beyond the scoreline. Managers are far better positioned to judge both the match and how individuals are faring. Is a player carrying a knock and not performing to his best? Is a defender getting pulled out of position by one particularly tricky attacker? Is the opposition's offside trap weak and liable to be sprung? These and a dozen other questions will be occupying the manager or coach's thoughts.

▲ In large squads, players, such as Celtic's John Hartson, here coming on for Henrik Larsson, have to accept a role on the bench.

◀ Substitute Teddy Sheringham prepares to enter the action in the 1999 Champions League final. It was an inspired decision by manager Sir Alex Ferguson (right) with Sheringham grabbing a vital goal (above).

MASTERCLASS
A winning attitude

Prepare for every game as if it is the biggest of the season.

As a substitute, warm up well before coming on. This will help you get up to speed in a game.

Don't ease up when your side are ahead. Too many games swing back the other way.

Accept the manager's decision to substitute you or play you in a different position.

Substitutions

Substitutions are a vital part of a manager's armoury. He can replace a player who is injured, not performing, or just needs a rest. A manager can also sacrifice a player in order to bring on another type of footballer. Two common substitutions are to bring off a striker when your team is winning by several goals, or to replace a defender with an extra attacker when your side is behind.

▲ Middlesbrough's Dean Windass (left) consoles Ray Parlour of Arsenal when Parlour is sent off.

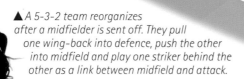

▲ A 5-3-2 team reorganizes after a midfielder is sent off. They pull one wing-back into defence, push the other into midfield and play one striker behind the other as a link between midfield and attack.

Changing tactics

Some coaches tinker constantly with tactics during a game – other coaches prefer to leave things pretty much as they are. But they all want their sides to get and maintain possession, to look secure in defence and be effective in attack. As a game develops, managers spot weaknesses in both teams and look to fix their own while exploiting those of the opposition. For example, a manager may pull a midfielder back to track and mark a dangerous opposition attacker who plays deep.

► Encouraging team-mates, as German goalkeeper Silke Rottenberg (top right) is doing, helps maintain confidence. The Korea Republic side (right) build morale as they huddle just before kick-off. Listening to the advice and support of team-mates is important for strong team spirit.

▲ Communication is vital in marshalling a team, as Fiorentina's Daniele Adani demonstrates.

A winning attitude

The best coaches in the world won't succeed unless their players have the right attitude. Coaches and managers seek to instill a winning attitude in their teams so that, even when things are going against them, the players continue to work hard to turn things around. But what is a winning attitude in practical terms? It involves keeping your confidence when your side is being overrun. It means not sniping at your own team-mates when they make a mistake, but encouraging them. Above all, it means concentrating and working not as individuals, but as a team.

"You can play any style that you like, the important thing is to create a strong group."
Cesare Maldini

A Pro's Life

Throughout the world, millions of children, teenagers and amateur adult players turn out for their local teams every week. Of these, it's a fairly safe bet that most, if not all, of them dream of one day getting paid for playing football and, eventually, reaching the very top of the professional game.

▲ Spectators watch a schoolboy game in East London's Victoria Park. Talented young players can give themselves a better chance of making the grade through hard work.

A long, long road

Gifted youngsters may be the best midfielders or strikers in their school, area or even region but they face a long, uphill path before they can join the top flight. Many never make the grade and others falter after joining a football club as a youth player, never completing the step up to the reserves and the first team. Disappointment is rife, but some players are lucky enough to be given a second chance.

► Dutch club Ajax is renowned for the quality of its youth academy, which has produced Johan Cruyff and Patrick Kluivert among many others. Here, former Holland star Arnold Muhren works with some of Ajax's youngsters.

▲ A club with a rich crop of youngsters has a greater chance of a rosy future. Manchester United's youth team of the early 1990s, pictured here after their 1993 FA Youth Cup final win, was captained by Gary Neville and also contained Paul Scholes, Nicky Butt and David Beckham.

Pro health

Top players are expensive assets, and clubs strive to keep them as healthy and fit as possible. The days of eating greasy food prior to a match are long gone. Diet and bodyweight are monitored carefully and foods packed with carbohydrates such as vegetables, pastas and rice are typical fare. Minor injuries or tiredness often result in a player losing form and possibly his place in the team. The biggest fear of most professionals is a major injury, which can keep them out for many months, or even end their career.

► Players receive immediate attention when they go down injured during a match. Here, Korea Republic's Woon Jae Lee is treated for a head injury during his side's 2001 Confederations Cup clash with Australia.

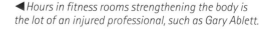

◄ Hours in fitness rooms strengthening the body is the lot of an injured professional, such as Gary Ablett.

◄ George Best, Britain's original footballing superstar, was one of the first to employ a business manager, pictured next to Best along with Best's secretary and chauffeur.

▲ Luis Figo attends a glamorous function with his wife, Helene. Top stars are major celebrities, often seen at gallery openings, movie premieres and exclusive parties.

Playing for a living

The majority of professional footballers earn a fraction of the likes of Rivaldo and Beckham. With relatively short playing careers and the threat of injury always present, more and more footballers use agents to negotiate good contracts and transfer deals on their behalf. Agents and certain freedom of work laws and court rulings have helped engineer far more player movement between clubs than ever before.

Rewards and responsibilities

The rewards for making it to the top are huge. Massive salaries, measured in tens of thousands of pounds per week, are just the start. Sponsorships and endorsements of a company's products can quickly make star players multi-millionaires, and that's before money from personal appearances, media work and cuts from a transfer deal. All this comes at a price, however. The pressure to perform and media intrusion are two of the negative aspects of a pro's life.

▲ Rivaldo collects his 1999 FIFA Player of the Year trophy at a glitzy awards ceremony held in Brussels.

◄ The money is great but most players dream of the glory of lifting a major trophy more than anything else. Here, Ronaldo kisses the Copa America trophy, which Brazil won in 1997.

► England internationals Rachel Brown and Karen Walker sign autographs for eager fans after a match.

Clubs and Supporters

The bond between supporters and their club is powerful and passionate. Fans may chant for a manager to leave or be unhappy with certain players or the current team but their love of the club itself remains. Many fans travel the world to show their undying support for their team.

▼ Club mascots often entertain the crowd before the game. This cartoon cat, called Gatton Gattoni, is Vicenza's mascot, the griffin bird is Perugia's.

An emotional rollercoaster

Whether it's your national team, your favourite professional club or a local amateur side you support, football matches generate a range of intense feelings. From the dreadful low of seeing your side knocked out of an important competition, to the incredible high of watching a spectacular winning goal by your team, the emotional rollercoaster ride you can experience is addictive – which is why most fans support the same club for their whole lifetime.

▲ The matchday programme is essential pre-match and half-time reading for many fans.

▶ Matchday sees the setting up of stalls near many football grounds. This laden stall outside Rome's Olympic Stadium is selling merchandise to passing Roma fans.

▼ Paris St Germain fans proclaim their support for their club via a sea of banners and flares during a Champions League encounter with Italian giants AC Milan.

Kitted out

To be a lifelong supporter of a football club is like being part of a close-knit tribe. Fans learn their own team's chants and songs, wear the club colours and buy many club-related products known as merchandise. Merchandising has become an important money-spinner for professional sides, with sales of shirts and other items through club shops often exceeding the money paid by spectators at the turnstiles.

FA CUP SEMI-FINAL
STOKE CITY
v ARSENAL
Villa Park, Saturday April 15th 1972, 3.00pm
Official Programme 10p

OFFICIAL PROGRAMME
SEASON, 1936-7

The big match

Many fans get excited long before the start of a new season or before an important match. Derby games, where a side plays their local rivals, tend to produce the most intense atmospheres. Derbies between Spanish rivals Real Madrid and Barcelona, Italian giants Internazionale and AC Milan, and the Scottish 'Old Firm' games between Celtic and Rangers are among the biggest clashes.

◀▼ Fans can generate an incredible atmosphere, few more so than the supporters of the Reggae Boyz – the nickname of Jamaica's national team (left). International games are an occasion to celebrate your country, as these face-painted USA supporters show (below).

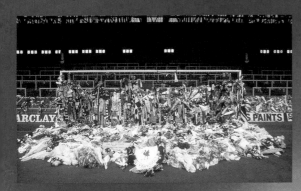

▲ Floral tributes left by supporters at Anfield, home of Liverpool FC. The tributes were in response to the 1989 Hillsborough tragedy in which 96 Liverpool fans died.

▲ Club shops sell shirts, clothing, souvenirs and other memorabilia to devoted supporters. This is the club shop of Japanese J-League side Yokohama Marinos.

Trouble and tragedy

Throughout football's history, there have been incidents of violence, accident and tragedy. The intense passion of some supporters can overstep the mark, turning to hatred, abuse and violence towards players, officials and, in particular, supporters of rival teams. Outbreaks of hooliganism and crowd trouble have blighted the game in Europe and South America, but more intelligent policing and the use of video cameras has led to many arrests. After a number of tragedies that saw people crushed or unable to escape fire, many stadiums have become less-crowded, all-seater venues with more attention paid to safety.

Football Media

Playing football and watching it live at the ground are only two of the ways in which supporters can immerse themselves in the game. Reading about football in newspapers and magazines, surfing the Internet, picking up scores from the radio or watching highlights on television all allow people to follow the sport they love.

The press

Pick up nearly any newspaper and you'll find that the back pages are devoted to sports news, interviews, results, rumours and gossip, with football tending to dominate on a day-to-day basis.

◀ Fans have a variety of options to choose from when it comes to finding out more about the game – magazines, newspapers and the traditional matchday programme.

▶ Websites, including this official site for Italian side Roma, allow fans to keep up to date with their club.

Some publications are often criticized for being too harsh on players, unsettling them with rumours of transfers and seeking to inflame disagreements and generate scandals. However, there's no doubt that the press stirs up enthusiasm and interest in the sport, allowing fans to obtain match reports and features on famous footballers and managers. Some fans of clubs, players or a particular competition produce publications for other fans. Known as fanzines, these publications are independent of clubs and offer ordinary supporters the chance to put their often critical opinions in print, thus reaching a wider audience.

▲ The first television filming of football came in 1936 when the BBC filmed a demonstration match at Arsenal's ground, Highbury, featuring Arsenal and Everton players.

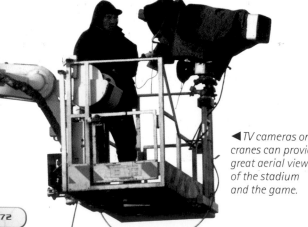

▶ Television coverage of the game has come on leaps and bounds since the early days, with viewers now able to call up a huge array of statistics.

◀ TV cameras on cranes can provide great aerial views of the stadium and the game.

◄Almost every angle is covered by TV cameras, including the bird's-eye view offered by this Goodyear 'blimp' airship.

Television coverage

Television more than any other arm of the media is responsible for the explosion of interest in football. The broadcasting of football today is a sophisticated operation involving many different camera angles, a soundtrack provided by commentators and pundits, and a whole host of behind-the-scenes technical staff.

New views and choices

Football has pushed television technology to provide new and improved ways of covering the game. The image-capture quality of cameras has increased, allowing crystal-clear slow-motion replays of even the fastest action. Cameras have also shrunk in size, so they can now be fitted into the back of the goal and other unusual places. The arrival of subscription and pay-per-view television via cable or satellite means that supporters have to pay larger sums to watch chosen games but in return more viewing options are being provided. Replays on demand and different camera angles can be selected, and match statistics can also be called up, just by pressing buttons on a remote control.

▲ Pitchside cameras help viewers feel even closer to the action and their heroes.

▲ Up in the commentary boxes, commentators call the game, explaining the action and who it involves.

► Giant screen technology shows instant replays of goals and other highlights to spectators.

Other media

Although television dominates, many fans rely on other media to follow games. Supporters can listen to live radio commentaries, or keep up to date with results via the Internet. The Net has thousands of official and unofficial websites dedicated to clubs, competitions and individual players. Chat rooms and mailing lists on the Net allow supporters to air their opinions and views. Such is the demand for up-to-the-minute football news and results that mobile phone users can receive the latest information through text messages.

◄ Pitchside reporters often grab short interviews with players and managers before, during and after a game.

◄ Terry Venables faces the press just after being appointed manager of the England team in 1994.

The press conference

Press conferences involve a footballer, manager or chairman of a club fielding questions from newspaper reporters, as well as television, radio and Internet journalists. Press conferences feed the media the latest information on transfers, new appointments and resignations, and help create the day's sports news.

◄Opened in 1903, Hampden Park was home to the world's biggest crowds for the first half of the 20th century. The stadium underwent major refurbishment in the 1970s and 1990s.

Stadiums

Just a place for spectators to watch football? Think again. Stadiums are the temples of football – each has its own special atmosphere and unique history. Here are just some of the most famous stadiums around the world.

Hampden Park

One of the first great stadiums, the home of the Scottish national side is also a club ground, built for and still used by the Queens Park football club. Until the 1950s, Hampden Park was the largest capacity football arena in the world. The 149,415 people who watched Scotland play England in 1937 is still a UK official record attendance. Refurbished as an all-seater stadium, Hampden's capacity is now 52,000.

◄Almost 200,000 people tried to cram into Wembley stadium for the 1923 FA Cup final between West Ham and Bolton. Its original capacity of 126,000 was reduced to 80,000 in more recent years.

Wembley

Built in just 300 days in 1923, the twin towers of north London's Wembley stadium were a stirring sight for visiting fans for over three quarters of a century. Wembley has been home to the England national side, the FA Cup final and, perhaps most famously of all, host to the 1966 World Cup final in which England beat West Germany 4-2. Wembley was closed in 2000 for major re-development.

San Siro

The Giuseppe Meazza stadium, better known as the San Siro, is home to two Italian Serie A giants. The San Siro started life in 1926 as the 35,000-capacity home of AC Milan. Milanese rivals Internazionale left their own stadium, Arena, to make the San Siro their home in 1955. The 85,000 all-seater ground has hosted two European Cup finals and games from the 1934 and 1990 World Cups.

▲ The 1990 renovations to the San Siro cost more than £50 million and added a third tier of seats to the ground, supported by 11 massive cylindrical towers.

Maracana

Based in Rio de Janeiro, Brazil, and home of the Brazilian national side, the Maracana is a vast arena. Opened in 1950 for the World Cup finals, the ground holds the official world record attendance when 199,854 spectators came to see Brazil play Uruguay. It also holds the world record club attendance of 177,656 for a game played in 1963 between Brazilian sides Flamingo and Fluminense.

▼ *The Maracana, also known as the Maracane and Estadio Mario Filho, now seats 120,000 spectators.*

▲ *Home to one of the world's biggest clubs, FC Barcelona, the Nou Camp, which means 'the new ground', hosted the opening of the 1982 World Cup.*

Nou Camp

The magnificent home stadium of Spanish club, Barcelona, the Nou Camp was opened in 1957 with a 90,000 capacity. This was later increased to a maximum capacity of around 115,000. Uniquely, the Nou Camp is connected via a walkway to a 16,500-seater stadium. This smaller ground is where Barcelona's reserve or nursery team plays in the lower divisions of the Spanish league.

Stade de France

Built on the site of a former gasworks specifically for the 1998 World Cup finals, the Stade de France is a state-of-the-art sports venue. Le Grand Stade, as it is popularly known, features a retractable lower tier, 36 lifts, 43 cafés and snack bars, 670 toilets, 17 shops and 454 floodlights. Built at a cost of more than £270 million, the stadium holds up to 80,000 spectators.

▼ *The 45,409-capacity Nagai stadium in Osaka, a major venue for the 2002 World Cup, was renovated in 1996.*

▶ *The crowd at the Stade de France use cards to spell out* Coupe de Monde *(World Cup) during the opening ceremony of the 1998 World Cup finals. France went on to win the final against Brazil.*

Nagai

Nagai stadium, one of a record 20 stadiums involved in the 2002 World Cup, co-hosted by Japan and South Korea, is the home of Japanese J-League club, Cerezo Osaka. Major international competitions such as the World Cup provide a major impetus to build new grounds and upgrade older ones such as Nagai stadium.

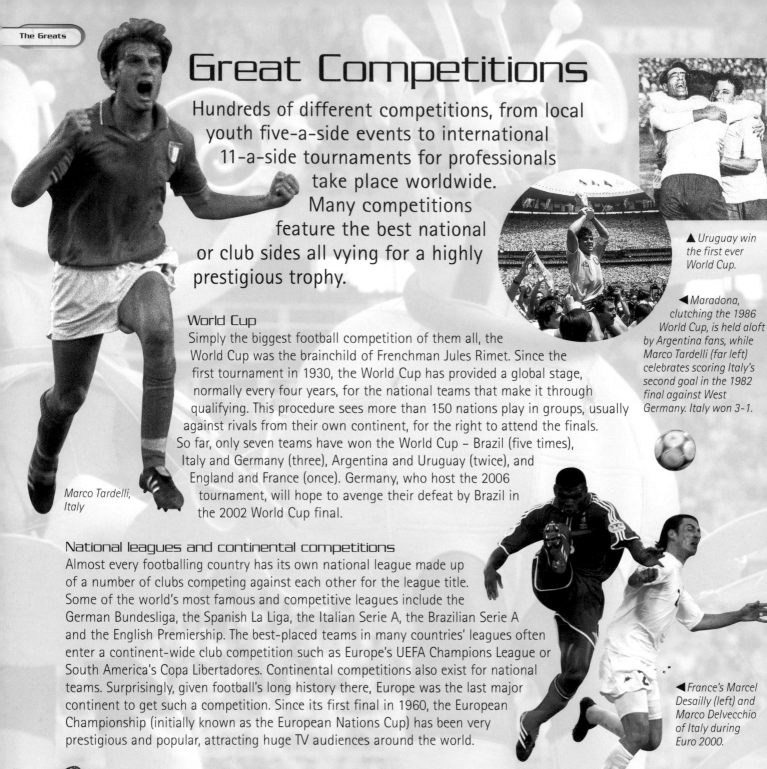

Great Competitions

Hundreds of different competitions, from local youth five-a-side events to international 11-a-side tournaments for professionals take place worldwide. Many competitions feature the best national or club sides all vying for a highly prestigious trophy.

Marco Tardelli, Italy

▲ *Uruguay win the first ever World Cup.*

◄ *Maradona, clutching the 1986 World Cup, is held aloft by Argentina fans, while Marco Tardelli (far left) celebrates scoring Italy's second goal in the 1982 final against West Germany. Italy won 3-1.*

World Cup

Simply the biggest football competition of them all, the World Cup was the brainchild of Frenchman Jules Rimet. Since the first tournament in 1930, the World Cup has provided a global stage, normally every four years, for the national teams that make it through qualifying. This procedure sees more than 150 nations play in groups, usually against rivals from their own continent, for the right to attend the finals. So far, only seven teams have won the World Cup – Brazil (five times), Italy and Germany (three), Argentina and Uruguay (twice), and England and France (once). Germany, who host the 2006 tournament, will hope to avenge their defeat by Brazil in the 2002 World Cup final.

National leagues and continental competitions

Almost every footballing country has its own national league made up of a number of clubs competing against each other for the league title. Some of the world's most famous and competitive leagues include the German Bundesliga, the Spanish La Liga, the Italian Serie A, the Brazilian Serie A and the English Premiership. The best-placed teams in many countries' leagues often enter a continent-wide club competition such as Europe's UEFA Champions League or South America's Copa Libertadores. Continental competitions also exist for national teams. Surprisingly, given football's long history there, Europe was the last major continent to get such a competition. Since its first final in 1960, the European Championship (initially known as the European Nations Cup) has been very prestigious and popular, attracting huge TV audiences around the world.

◄ *France's Marcel Desailly (left) and Marco Delvecchio of Italy during Euro 2000.*

▼ *Rivaldo (far left) and, next to him, Ronaldo are part of the throng of Brazilian players enjoying their 1999 Copa America success. Surprisingly, this was only the sixth time Brazil had won.*

Copa America

The first continental competition for national teams began in 1910 and was named the Copa America – the South American Championship. A mere 8,000 spectators watched Argentina beat fierce rivals Uruguay 4-1 in the final. Uruguay took their revenge in the second competition, held some six years later in 1916, as they defeated Argentina to lift the trophy. Between 1959 and 1987, the tournament was usually played once every four years. In the years either side of these dates, the tournament tended to take place every two years. Argentina and Uruguay have dominated, with 15 and 14 wins respectively. Brazil, Peru, Paraguay and Bolivia have also been winners. Host nation Colombia beat Mexico in the final of the 2002 competition.

African Nations Cup

The African Nations Cup started in 1957 with just three teams – Egypt, Ethiopia and Sudan. Egypt emerged as winners. Since its small-scale beginnings, the competition has grown in size and importance. South Africa was re-admitted into African football in 1992 and, in 1996, the number of teams contesting the trophy was increased from 12 to 16. 12 different nations have won the tournament, Ghana and Egypt being the most successful with four victories each. Both the 2000 tournament, co-hosted by Ghana and Nigeria, and the 2002 tournament, held in Mali, saw narrow victories on penalties after extra time for Cameroon's "Indomitable Lions".

▲ Cameroon's Lucien Mettomo receives the African Nations Cup after his team beat Nigeria in the 2000 final.

Asian Cup

The Asian Cup started in 1956 and has boomed in quality and popularity since its early days. The 12 founder members of the Asian Football Confederation have now expanded to some 45 countries – more than half of the world's football-playing peoples. Recent tournaments have involved major tussles between Far Eastern nations, such as China and Japan, and teams from the Middle East, such as Kuwait, United Arab Emirates and Iran. The 2000 Asian Cup final, held in Lebanon, saw Japan clinch a tense 1-0 victory over a strong Saudi Arabian team.

▲ Japan line up with the Asian Cup trophy after their narrow win over Saudi Arabia in 2000.

▶ Cameroon's Joel Epalle (left) and Puyol of Spain chase the ball in the 2000 Olympics final.

Olympic Games

Football was played at the first modern Olympics, held in Athens in 1896, and it remained a demonstration sport at the Games until 1908. Before being overshadowed by the arrival of the World Cup in 1930, it was the only global football competition around. From 1952 to 1988, nearly every winner came from Eastern Europe. The 1990s saw the introduction of women's football at the Games, and the emergence of African nations, with Nigeria in 1996, and then Cameroon in 2000, both winning the final.

▲ USA's Tiffeny Milbrett (left) and Norway's Goeril Kringen at the 2000 Olympics.

▼ Canada's Josa De Vos and Craig Forrest (left) with the 2000 CONCACAF trophy.

CONCACAF Gold Cup

In 1941, a tournament for the football-playing countries of Central America was devised. Now known as the CONCACAF Gold Cup, it has been held in various formats and guises and has occasionally involved invited guest teams such as Brazil. At times, teams from North America have been included as well. In 1991, for example, the USA recorded its first victory in the competition, beating Honduras on penalties in the final. With ten wins – a tally that includes victories in eight of the first 11 competitions – Costa Rica have lifted the trophy more than any other nation. In recent times, Mexico has dominated, winning three tournaments on the trot between 1993 and 1998. Canada were the victors in 2000, beating Colombia 2-0 in the final and notching up their first international tournament win since the 1904 Olympic Games.

"They were simply a great team and they took us apart..."

Sir Stanley Matthews about the 1953 Hungary team

Great Games 1

England 3 Hungary 6, friendly, 1953

Despite England's lacklustre performance in the 1950 World Cup (the first time they entered the competition), many people still believed they were one of the best teams in the world.

A friendly match at Wembley against a gifted and tactically brilliant Hungarian side, headed by the attacking genius of Ferenc Puskas, quickly shattered that illusion.

▲ An England cross is cut out by Hungarian goalkeeper Gyula Grosics.

▶ Hungary's number ten, Ferenc Puskas, turns to the crowd to celebrate another goal for his team.

Magic Magyars

From the first minute, the England side, boasting stars such as Stanley Matthews, Billy Wright and Tom Finney, were outclassed and outplayed. The fluid Hungarian side, dubbed the 'Magic Magyars', launched wave after wave of ferocious attacks. The rigid English tactics couldn't handle the sublime skills and movement of Kocsis and Puskas, or those of the midfielder Nandor Hidegkuti, who scored a hat-trick.

◀ England's goalkeeper Gil Merrick comes out to block a shot from the boot of Sandor Kocsis.

A class act

If Hungary hadn't eased up in the last 20 minutes of the game, they may have added three or four more goals to their tally. The Hungarian victory at Wembley was no fluke. Six months later, an England side with seven changes travelled to Hungary for a re-match. England were thumped 7-1.

Real Madrid 7 Eintracht Frankfurt 3, European Cup Final, 1960

One of the finest exhibitions of football ever seen between two teams hell-bent on winning the European Cup was watched by 127,621 people at Hampden Park in Glasgow, Scotland. Eintracht Frankfurt who had demolished their semi-final opponents Glasgow Rangers, opened the scoring and dominated the first quarter of the game. Real Madrid then burst into life, with their two outstanding players Alfredo di Stefano and Puskas running rings around the German team. The great vision, swift movement and superlative ball skills captivated the crowd and took Real Madrid from one goal down to 7-3 in style. Di Stefano completed his hat-trick in the 74th minute, just two minutes after Puskas had hit his fourth goal.

◀ Puskas scores Real Madrid's fourth goal with an effortless kick from the penalty spot.

▲ The Real Madrid side celebrate their sensational 7-3 victory over Eintracht Frankfurt to win the European Cup.

Non-stop action

Eintracht's commitment to attacking was as much a factor in this spellbinding match as the Spanish side's dazzling play. The German side didn't give up easily – in the second half they hit the woodwork twice and twice put the ball in the back of the net. But it wasn't enough to prevent Real Madrid's onslaught.

◄ *Real Madrid goalkeeper Dominguez makes another save as Eintracht Frankfurt try to get back in the game.*

Brazil 4 Italy 1, World Cup final, 1970

The 1970 World Cup in Mexico, the first to feature red and yellow cards and substitutes, was a wonderful display of high-class football and epic games. It culminated in a final that saw what is considered the finest team display by an international side. That side was Brazil. Their opponents Italy were on top form as well. Although Italy had beaten the fancied West German side in the semi-finals 4-3, the talents of, among others, Pelé, Rivelino, and Jairzinho proved just too much for them.

◄ *Jairzinho makes a run behind Italian player, Giacinto Facchetti. Jairzinho scored in every round of the World Cup, including the final.*

Pelé scores first

Pelé opened the Brazilian account with a superbly taken header in the 19th minute. But a sloppy Brazilian backpass was exploited by Boninsegna who equalized for Italy. In the second half, Gerson put Brazil ahead again, with a brilliant individual effort. Picking up the ball 35 metres from goal, he changed direction to beat one defender before unleashing a precise and devastating shot.

► *Pelé celebrates after scoring the opening goal for Brazil. It was the last international match in which he played.*

On top of the world

The remainder of the second half was a one-sided display of outstanding football, with the Brazilians dominating the game and scoring twice more. The final goal was pure genius. With five minutes to go, a wonderful series of passes by the Brazilian forwards resulted in Pelé rolling the ball out to his right. Timing his run to perfection, Carlos Alberto connected with the ball first time, thundering a shot into the Italian net. It was a fitting climax to the game. Satellite broadcasting, used for the first time during this World Cup, allowed millions of people around the world to watch one of the greatest of all international matches.

▲ *Carlos Alberto seals Brazil's 4-1 victory with a stunning drive beyond the reach of Italian goalkeeper Albertosi.*

Great Games 2

Congo 3 Mali 2, African Nations Cup final, 1972

Football in Africa is not a recent phenomenon. Although the World Cup and Olympic exploits of teams such as Nigeria and Cameroon during the 1990s are well known, African football has a long history. The African Nations Cup, which started in 1957 and is the equivalent of the European Championships, has produced some classic games. One of the greatest is the 1972 final, held in Cameroon, between two very attacking sides – Congo and Mali.

▲ *François M'Pelé, who scored for Congo in the final, played for the French side Paris St Germain during the 1970s.*

▲ *A Mali defender wins a challenge for the ball with M'Pelé. As runners up, this remains Mali's highest achievement to date in the African Nations Cup.*

No let up

Mali dominated the first half. Only a series of acrobatic saves from Congo goalkeeper Masima kept Mali at bay, although they managed to take the lead right at the end of the first half. Congo surged forward in the second half with M'Bono scoring two goals in two minutes. M'Pelé added a third and the game looked over until Mali scored their second with 15 minutes to go. Despite a grandstand finish with both sides playing wonderfully fluid football, the score remained 3-2 to Congo.

West Germany 2 Holland 1, World Cup final, 1974

Although billed as a battle between Dutch maestro Johan Cruyff and brilliant German tactician Franz Beckenbauer, the match was in fact a fascinating and highly skilled encounter between two teams at their peak. The game began explosively, with Cruyff brought down in the German penalty area soon after kick-off. The penalty was converted by Johan Neeskens. The Dutch continued to dominate the game with elegant and fluid movement focused around Cruyff, Neeskens and Johnny Rep.

▲ *With under two minutes on the clock, Johan Cruyff (on the ground, right) is brought down by Uli Hoeness. The resulting penalty, scored by Johan Neeskens, is the fastest goal in a World Cup final.*

Enter 'The Bomber'

Superb defending, and outstanding goalkeeping from Sepp Maier, prevented Holland from netting the vital second goal. The Germans made the Dutch pay for their lack of killer instinct by equalizing with a penalty. Then, in the 43rd minute, the German striker Gerd Müller, nicknamed 'Der Bomber' scored a second for his side with a glorious individual effort.

Dutch pressure

The Dutch pressed furiously for an equalizer, but Sepp Maier, the goalkeeper of the tournament, continued to thwart them. As more space opened up, West Germany also had their chances with Müller particularly unlucky when he had a goal disallowed for offside, although replays confirmed he was onside.

▶ *Despite giving away a penalty, West Germany and Bayern Munich forward Uli Hoeness, just 22 years old at the time, played an important part in the German victory.*

Revenge

The 2-1 final scoreline meant that West Germany were crowned world champions. Unfortunately for the Dutch supporters and players, they had to wait some 14 years for victory over the Germans. Their Euro '88 side, boasting legendary players such as Ruud Gullit and Marco Van Basten, finally put to rest painful memories of their 1974 World Cup loss.

◄ *The Dutch defence crumbles as Gerd Müller displays dazzling footwork before firing the ball home with his right foot.*

► *French midfielder, Alain Giresse (right) formed a magnificent partnership with Jean Tigana, Luis Fernandez and Michel Platini throughout the tournament.*

France 3 Portugal 2, European Championships, 1984

This enthralling semi-final was the game that put the European Championships on the map. The French midfield of Jean Tigana, Alain Giresse and Michel Platini controlled much of the match with a wonderful display of passing and movement. At half-time, the much-fancied French team were 1-0 up thanks to Domergue. During the second half, the French couldn't consolidate their lead. Attack after attack was repelled, with the Portuguese goalkeeper Manuel Bento making some great saves. Then in the 73rd minute, Rui Jordao equalized for Portugal, shocking the 55,000 crowd packed into Marseille's Velodrome stadium.

► *Michel Platini makes one of his trademark runs through the Portuguese defence. Platini's haul of nine goals in the tournament remains a European Championships record.*

▲ *French defender Maxime Bossis falls to the ground. The French victory in the finals helped ease memories of Bossis' missed penalty, which had lost France their World Cup semi-final against West Germany two years before.*

At the last minute

Extra time came and the game opened up further with wave after wave of attacks by both sides. Portugal took the lead with striker Jordao scoring again, but France pulled back with a goal from Domergue. Another dreaded penalty shootout looked inevitable. Then, in the very last minute of extra time, Jean Tigana played a cross into the penalty area. It was met by Platini who struck it sweetly into the back of the net, securing victory seconds before the final whistle. Four days later, France beat Spain in the final 2-0 to win their first-ever international competition. Platini was made player of the tournament.

Great Games 3

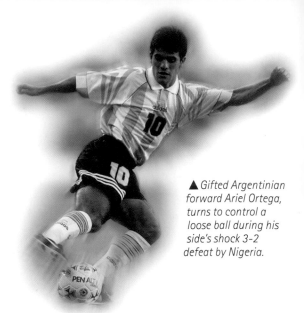

Argentina 2 Nigeria 3, Olympic final, 1996

Inspired attacking from both sides made for a thrilling match, full of goalmouth incidents. The game began badly for Nigeria. With less than two minutes on the clock, poor defending allowed Argentina's Claudio Lopez plenty of space to head home the opening goal. But Nigeria weren't a team to give up easily. In a dramatic semi-final against Brazil they had come from behind to beat the South Americans 4-3, and now in the final they fought back with great determination and flair.

▲ Gifted Argentinian forward Ariel Ortega, turns to control a loose ball during his side's shock 3-2 defeat by Nigeria.

▲ Nigerian midfielder, Jay-Jay Okocha, makes a challenge on the Argentinian player, Bassedas. Okocha has played in Nigeria, France, Turkey and Germany.

On the attack

Celestine Babayaro's equalizing header was as impressive as his celebration – a spectacular double somersault. However, the Argentinians struck back with a penalty taken by Hernan Crespo. With 15 minutes to go, Amokachi latched on to the ball and flicked it over the Argentinian goalkeeper. The final appeared to be heading for extra time when Nigeria was awarded a free-kick wide out on the left.

Going for gold

The Argentinian defence tried to catch Nigeria offside, but Emmanuel Amunike beat the trap and volleyed home the winner in the 89th minute. The final whistle was met with wild celebrations. Nigeria had become the first African nation to win a major international cup competition.

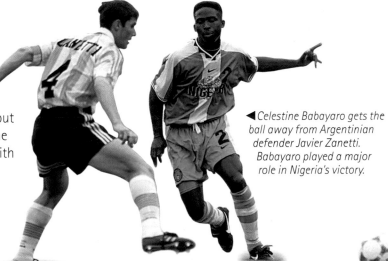

◀ Celestine Babayaro gets the ball away from Argentinian defender Javier Zanetti. Babayaro played a major role in Nigeria's victory.

China 5 Norway 0, Women's World Cup semi-final, 1999

Along with the eventual winners – USA – Norway and China were far and away the most fancied sides in the 1999 World Cup finals. This semi-final clash was a contrast in styles between the determined and defensively strong Norwegian team and a Chinese side that relied on pace and close-range passing. China ran riot. The blistering speed and superb movement of their team proved far too much for a tough Norwegian side that started the match as favourites in many commentators' eyes. China made a fairytale start to the game when striker Sun Wen scored in the third minute.

◀ Ying Liu, one of China's talented strikers, shows she's equally adept at defending as she makes a robust sliding challenge on the veteran Norwegian captain Linda Medalen.

Unstoppable

Liu Ailing doubled the lead with a blistering right-footed volley 11 minutes later. Ailing, superb with either foot, scored her second, a left-footed volley, after a corner wasn't properly cleared by the Norwegian defence. Norway threatened the Chinese goal on a number of occasions in the second half but one of the best goalkeepers in the women's game, Gao Hong, pulled off three spectacular saves to foil them. China retaliated with a fourth in the 63rd minute from yet another volley, this time by defender Fan Yunjie. Sun Wen's 72nd minute penalty made her joint top scorer for the tournament, along with the Brazilian Sissi, and completed the 5-0 victory, equalling Norway's worst ever defeat.

▲ The Chinese players celebrate another goal in their devastating 5-0 victory over Norway.

▼ Slobodan Komljenovic (right) celebrates a 2-1 lead six minutes into the second half with goalscorer Dejan Govedarica.

▲ Abelardo (left) and Mijatovic tangle for possession of the ball.

▲ Alfonso (left) tackles Yugoslavian defender, Sinisa Mihalovic.

Brilliant strikes

Early in the second half, Yugoslavia took the lead again. Dejan Govedarica, a half-time substitute for Vladimir Jugovic, powered a superb strike from the edge of the penalty area. A minute later, Pedro Munitis eclipsed Govedarica's goal, firing in a wonderful curling shot. With the game poised at 2-2, it appeared the turning point had come in the 63rd minute when Jokanovic was sent off. Spain now had the advantage.

Last-minute thriller

In an earlier group match against Slovenia, Yugoslavia had made an incredible comeback from 3-0 down, again with only ten men. True to form, against the Spanish side, Yugoslavia scored next when a goalmouth scramble saw Komljenovic slam the ball home. Yugoslavia fought desperately hard to protect their lead and appeared to have secured a wonderful victory. Into injury time, and the Spanish looked to be heading home before a disputed penalty, converted by Mendieta, appeared to have created the fairest of results – a 3-3 draw. But this epic game had yet more drama, when in the dying seconds, Alfonso volleyed home the winner for Spain. The Yugoslavs were downcast but it turned out that both they and Spain advanced to the next stage.

Spain 4 Yugoslavia 3, Euro 2000

This pulsating contest proved the undoubted highlight of Euro 2000 and a contender for the best-ever European Championships game. It started as an important group encounter with neither side certain of qualifying for the next stage. Spain looked to be the sharper side at first, carving out a number of attacking chances but were hit by a classic counter-attack that saw Savo Milosevic head the first goal for Yugoslavia. Spain pressed forward in numbers and Raul's darting run let Alfonso equalize.

"The difference between heaven and hell is one minute."
Josep Guardiola after the Spain vs Yugoslavia match.

▲ Alfonso scores the winning goal for Spain with a well-hit volley in the dying moments of a thrilling game.

The Great Players 1

Alfredo Di Stefano (born 1926, Buenos Aires, Argentina)
Di Stefano (right) joined his father's old club, River Plate, as a teenager and soon became part of an extremely successful forward line known as 'La Maquina' – The Machine. In 1953, he moved to the legendary Spanish team Real Madrid, which dominated European football in the 1950s and early 1960s. A centre-forward, Di Stefano was also brilliant at defending, tackling, creating chances for other players, as well as scoring many superbly taken goals himself. Real Madrid player and coach Miguel Munoz summed up his contribution to the game – "The greatness of Di Stefano was that, with him in your side, you had two players in every position."

Lev Yashin (born 1929, Moscow, former Soviet Union. Died 1990)
Just pipping Gordon Banks, Lev Yashin (left) is still regarded as football's greatest goalkeeper. Nicknamed the 'Black Panther' for his incredible agility and awesome saves, he had an almost supernatural anticipation of where the ball would next appear. During his 20-year career at Moscow Dynamo (where he had originally started out as the club's ice-hockey goaltender), the team won the Supreme League title six times and the Soviet Cup twice. He also won 78 caps for the Soviet Union. Records are sketchy but Yashin is believed to have saved more than 150 penalties in his illustrious career. In 1968, he was awarded the Order of Lenin, at that time the Soviet Union's highest honour.

Pelé (Edson Arantes do Nascimento, born 1940, Tres Coracoes, Brazil)
If any player deserved a ten out of ten over a long career, it has to be the man who always wore that number for his main club, Santos, and for his national team, Brazil. Pelé had it all – pace, strength, creativity, breathtaking vision and skills to match. At the age of 17, he became an instant celebrity, scoring six goals for Brazil's 1958 World-Cup-winning side. It was the first of three World Cups that Pelé helped to win for his country. The last, in 1970, featured some of his finest moments – outrageous dummies, flicks, passes and shots few others would have attempted. Pelé played 93 internationals for Brazil, with a remarkable tally of 77 goals. When Pelé retired from Santos in 1974 after 18 years, the club removed the number ten shirt from their team as a tribute. He later came out of retirement to help promote professional soccer in the United States, playing for the New York Cosmos, before retiring for good in 1977. In 1994, Pelé was appointed Brazil's Minister of Sport.

Eusebio da Silva Ferreira (born 1942, Lourenco Marques, Mozambique)
Eusebio played his early football in Mozambique, at that time a Portuguese colony. Although groomed to play for the famous Portuguese club Sporting Lisbon, he was snapped up by their great rivals Benfica. He scored more than 300 goals in his 15-year career at Benfica and the club won major honours in all but two of those years. Blessed with an explosive right foot, there was a good deal more to the 'Black Pearl's' game than powerful shooting. Wonderfully skilled in all areas of attacking play, he was admired for his sportsmanship, even in the tensest encounters. In 1965, he was voted European Footballer of the Year. The following year, Eusebio was the leading scorer in the World Cup with nine goals to his credit.

Franz Beckenbauer
(born 1945, Munich, Germany)
An outstanding defender, Beckenbauer revolutionized the position of sweeper. Originally an ultra-defensive position, he made the role of sweeper into an exciting way of turning defence into attack. In game after game for Bayern Munich and his national side, West Germany, the player nicknamed 'Kaiser Franz' had a match-winning impact, creating hundreds of scoring opportunities for his team-mates. He didn't hold back from making shots on goal himself and put away 44 goals for Bayern. Beckenbauer was capped 103 times for West Germany, and under his captaincy, the team triumphed in the 1974 World Cup. He was appointed manager of the national team in 1984 and steered them to victory over Argentina in the 1990 World Cup final.

George Best (born 1946, Belfast, Northern Ireland)
One of the most extravagantly gifted players to grace the game, George Best shared with Pelé attacking vision, brilliant goalscoring skills and an eye for the unexpected or outrageous. Superb with both feet and fearless in the tackle, Best was a supreme dribbler of the ball. He was also a deadly finisher with 137 goals for Manchester United, the club he joined as a teenager. He was instrumental in United's European Cup victory over Benfica in 1968. His national side, Northern Ireland, never made it to the World Cup finals. Although he made a number of comebacks in both Britain and North America, the player dubbed 'the fifth Beatle' was never the same after he sensationally quit Manchester United in 1973. The pressure of fame and being Britain's first footballing superstar had sadly taken its toll.

The Great Players 2

Johan Cruyff (born 1947, Amsterdam, Holland)
One of the greatest of European footballers, Cruyff (left) was a key player in the Dutch revolution known as 'total football'. This involved players changing positions with breathtaking speed and effectiveness. Cruyff, three times European Footballer of the Year, displayed sublime ball skills and, although a centre-forward, he was equally effective in midfield or on the wings. He enjoyed huge success at the Dutch club Ajax where he was instrumental in the team winning three European Cups. In 1973, he moved to Barcelona where he helped the Spanish side win a number of league and cup titles. Cruyff returned to Ajax and then Barcelona as manager, taking both teams to victory in European cup competitions.

Diego Maradona (born 1960, Buenos Aires, Argentina)
A superb goalscorer with beautiful technical skills, Maradona was *the* player of the 1980s. Highlights of his career include winning two Italian league titles with Napoli and his play in the 1986 World Cup, when he transformed a solid Argentinian side into world beaters. During the tournament, Maradona provided a serious contender for the greatest goal ever – against England during the quarter-finals (earlier in the same game, he infamously used his hand to score a goal). Despite leading Argentina to the 1990 World Cup finals, where they finished as runners-up (losing 1-0 to West Germany), Maradona's later years were sadly dogged by failed drug tests and disappointing comebacks.

Michel Platini (born 1955, Joeuf, France)
One of the most effective midfielders the game has ever seen, Platini (below) captained the French side to the 1982 World Cup semi-finals and to victory in the 1984 European Championships. Supremely creative, Platini was dazzling in attack or hovering around the midfield, hitting deadly accurate 40-metre passes. Playing for the great Italian side Juventus, he was Serie A's leading scorer and was crowned European Footballer of the Year in 1983, 1984 and 1985. In 1992, five years after retiring, he became manager of the French national side and later headed France's successful bid to host the World Cup in 1998.

George Weah (born 1966, Monrovia, Liberia)

Born in the small African nation of Liberia, Weah played for four clubs in Africa before Arsene Wenger, the manager of Monaco, brought the 22-year-old forward to Europe in 1988. Weah proved instrumental to Monaco winning the 1991 French league championship. He transferred to Paris SG and helped them win the league title in 1994, and then moved to the celebrated Italian team Milan. Both powerful and graceful, Weah was also a devastating finisher. In 1995, he won a unique treble – African Player of the Year, European Footballer of the Year and FIFA Player of the Year. He has invested much of his footballing fortune into helping charities and developing the game back in Liberia.

Mariel Margaret 'Mia' Hamm
(born 1972, Alabama, USA)

The most famous player in women's football, Mia Hamm was the youngest ever American international when she debuted in 1987 at the age of 15. She dominated the 1990s as the game's most inspirational and devastating attacker, with more than 100 goals to her credit, helping the USA to win both Olympic and World Cup titles. She was voted US soccer's Female Athlete of the Year an unprecedented five years running, from 1994 to 1998. Usually playing as a forward, Hamm took over in goal during the 1995 Women's World Cup, after the regular goalkeeper, Briana Scurry, was sent off.

Zinedine Zidane (born 1972, Marseilles, France)

The son of Algerian immigrants, Zidane has captivated spectators around the world with his brilliant performances. He helped France win the 1998 World Cup (including two goals scored in the final against Brazil) and the 2000 European Championships. Blessed with a delicate touch and quick acceleration, 'Zizou' as he is known to his fans, is at his best when making space for himself in a crowded midfield or on the edge of the opposition's penalty area. He made his name playing for the French club Bordeaux, where he won France's Player of the Year award in 1996, before moving to the Italian side, Juventus. Voted World Footballer of the Year in 2001, Zidane is one of the most highly sought-after players in the game. In July 2001, he went from Juventus to Real Madrid for a world record fee of £48 million.

British Football

Football in Britain has a long history and there have been many changes to the game's rules and the structure of the competitions. Today, the two professional British leagues – in Scotland and in England – feature three divisions topped by a Premiership or Premier League division. Promotion and relegation allow clubs to rise or fall between the divisions, and give semi-professional and amateur clubs a chance to step up to the big time.

A golden age of managers

Britain has produced more than its fair share of famous managers, from Herbert Chapman who guided Arsenal to dominance in the 1920s and 1930s, to Sir Alex Ferguson, Martin O'Neill, and England supremos Terry Venables and Bobby Robson, both of whom enjoyed great managerial success abroad.

The period from 1950 to 1980, however, threw up more successful and famous club managers than any other period in British footballing history. Men such as Bill Nicholson at Tottenham Hotspur, Sir Matt Busby at Manchester United, Jock Stein at Celtic and Bill Shankly and Bob Paisley at Liverpool, enjoyed long and illustrious careers helping to shape and define their respective clubs.

Bill Nicholson joined Spurs as a player way back in 1937. He was a superb tactician and coach and led the north-London side to the first European trophy won by a British club – beating Atletico Madrid 5-1 in the 1963 Cup-Winners' Cup final – as well as the league and FA Cup double in 1961.

Sir Matt Busby is credited with creating the Manchester United people know today. The Scot took charge in the 1940s, and by the time he retired in 1969, he had created several complete generations of gifted, attacking teams. One of the most exciting was his late-1960s side which, with Bobby Charlton, Denis Law and George Best, became, in 1968, the first English team to win the European Cup.

Bill Shankly was a tough, no-nonsense manager possessing huge charisma and a gruff wit that has made him the most quoted of footballing men. One of five brothers who all played professional football, Shankly took the reins at Liverpool when they were a lowly second division side. By the time he handed over to Bob Paisley, Shankly had transformed the team into a winning machine. Liverpool remain the most successful British club abroad, and the most successful at home in England, with a record 18 league titles.

Jock Stein, another Scot, managed Leeds, Dunfermline, Hibs and the Scottish national team but it was his 13-year stint as manager of Celtic for which he will be most remembered. In that time, Stein completely overhauled the Scottish club, turning them into one of the great European sides. His brand of attacking, skilful play powered Celtic to the first European Cup win by a British side in 1967, and to nine Scottish league titles in a row, a record later equalled by Rangers.

Brian Clough, with his abrasive, unpredictable manner and innovative coaching style, was never far from the headlines during the 1970s and 1980s. A prolific goalscorer until his playing career was cut short by injury, Clough had a deep understanding of football and was a superb motivator. He was capable of boosting relatively modest players as well as clubs such as Derby and Nottingham Forest to league titles and European glory.

British is best?

Despite acknowledging the superiority of many foreign clubs and national sides, Britain proved slow to accept foreign managers. In 1990, there was ridicule and contempt when Slovak Dr Jozef Venglos took over at Aston Villa.

Just over a decade later, much has changed, with foreign managers of the calibre of Arsenal's French boss Arsène Wenger, Italian Claudio Ranieri of Chelsea, and England's first-ever foreign coach, the Swede Sven-Goran Eriksson.

The romance of the Cup

The year 1871 marked the start of the first and oldest surviving knockout competition, the FA Cup. Since that time, the Cup has thrown up a thousand stories and hundreds of heroes.

Some critics say that the European glamour and financial rewards of the Champions League have led to the FA Cup losing some of its appeal. Try telling that to the supporters whose club has just reached the final, or the millions of TV viewers, not just in Britain but all over the world, who tune in to the most-watched domestic competition on the planet.

Although for the big boys in the top two divisions the FA Cup starts with the third round, traditionally played in January, you have to go all the way back to the previous August to see the competition's true start. Qualifying rounds, involving hundreds of non-league teams, are played to give a relative handful of these sides a tilt at second and third division opposition in the first round. This is where the fur really starts to fly. The FA Cup is famous for its giant-killing acts where teams from lower tiers triumph over more illustrious opponents. It's a very rare first round that doesn't see one or more non-league sides beat league opposition and make the sporting headlines the next day.

The last 64

By the time the Premiership and Division One sides join the fray, the competition is already down to the last 64 teams. The growing gulf in finance between those at the very top and the rest has made it increasingly hard for giant-killing to occur. A top-flight player's boot-sponsorship deal can be worth more than an entire opposition team, yet plenty of Premiership and Division One clubs are frequently taken to a replay. Over the years, there have been some stunning shock wins. In 1972, Southern League side Hereford United thrilled a nation by beating first division giants Newcastle United 2-1. Non-league Yeovil have the most impressive of all giant-killing records, beating league opposition a record 18 times in the FA Cup.

As the rounds progress and numbers reduce, many epic struggles occur before wildly passionate crowds. Division One clubs frequently beat Premiership outfits, league leaders often lose to lower-placed rivals, and a seemingly endless stream of stories results. Eventually, it comes down to four teams to contest the semi-finals, held at neutral venues, for the right to play in the final. For almost 80 years, that meant a match at Wembley, but the closing of the famous stadium for re-development has deprived the FA Cup final of its traditional venue. Cardiff's magnificent Millennium Stadium has proved a fitting backdrop to finals from 2001 onwards. Arsenal featured in the 2001, 2002 and 2003 finals, losing to Liverpool in 2001 but winning the next two.

Recent changes and innovations

The 1958 FA-Cup-winning side Bolton Wanderers cost a total of £110 to assemble, none of the players requiring a transfer fee and each player joining the club for a £10 signing-on fee. Today, many players in the Scottish Premier League and the Premiership earn 200 or more times that every week. Transfers have sky-rocketed into the tens of millions bracket, and even relatively ordinary footballers can command a transfer fee of £3-4 million and wages of £5,000-£15,000 a week. Who pays for all of this? Most revenue is now generated away from the actual match in

sponsorship deals, merchandise sales and television rights. A number of football clubs have floated on the Stock Exchange to raise millions of pounds. But football becoming big business is not the only innovation to occur in the British professional game in the past 20 years.

In 1987, a major change to the way teams are promoted in the English leagues was introduced in the form of the play-offs. The play-offs see the third- to sixth-placed teams in a division (except Division Three, where it is the teams placed fourth to seventh) play a semi-final and final game at the end of the regular season for the right to be promoted to the next division. The number of teams involved in the play-offs is expected to rise to six in the 2003/2004 season. Supporters of a side that has suffered a defeat in a play-off final know how heartbreaking this can be, but in general the play-offs have been well received. As well as generating a little extra revenue, they also help maintain interest throughout the long season. In fact, attendance at matches reached an incredible 38-year high in 2002/2003, with over 14.8 million spectators in divisions one, two and three.

The top divisions of both the Scottish and English leagues broke away from league control in the 1990s. Although still linked to the other divisions by promotion and relegation, the Scottish Premier League (SPL) and the Premiership negotiate their own sponsorship and TV rights and, as a result, money has flooded into the top clubs' coffers. While Celtic and Rangers have traditionally dominated the Scottish football scene, a similar trend appears to be occurring south of the border, where a small handful of clubs with greater financial clout is dominating the top three or four places of the league.

Foreign invaders

Players from Scotland, Northern Ireland, Wales and the Republic of Ireland have always passed relatively freely between the English and Scottish leagues. Yet, before the late 1980s, players from outside the British Isles were relatively rare. Ipswich Town's talented Dutch pair of Arnold Muhren and Frans Thijssen, and Spurs' inspired signing of Argentinian duo Osvaldo Ardiles and Ricky Villa were pioneering foreign arrivals. Today, the number of foreigners in British football is measured in hundreds, with high-calibre players all choosing to ply their trade here.

Although it's arguable whether it is the very best league in the world, there's no doubt the Premiership offers a vibrant, all-action style of football, which makes for many incidents, goals and highlights. It is certainly one of the most exciting and most watched competitions in world football.

Stats and Facts

Statistics and records are a vital part of the game for supporters, commentators and even managers and these days you can buy whole books dedicated to facts and figures. Below are some of the most important and fascinating British football stats available.

LEAGUE CHAMPIONS

In Scotland, two teams have dominated the league – Celtic with 39 titles and Rangers with 49. In England, despite Manchester United's prominence in the 1990s, Liverpool hold the record with 18 league titles. Below are the post-war records.

England

2003 Manchester United
2002 Arsenal
2001 Manchester United
2000 Manchester United
1999 Manchester United
1998 Arsenal
1997 Manchester United
1996 Manchester United
1995 Blackburn Rovers
1994 Manchester United
1993 Manchester United
1992 Leeds United
1991 Arsenal
1990 Liverpool
1989 Arsenal
1988 Liverpool
1987 Everton
1986 Liverpool
1985 Everton
1984 Liverpool
1983 Liverpool
1982 Liverpool
1981 Aston Villa
1980 Liverpool
1979 Liverpool
1978 Nottingham Forest
1977 Liverpool
1976 Liverpool
1975 Derby County
1974 Leeds United
1973 Liverpool
1972 Derby County
1971 Arsenal
1970 Everton
1969 Leeds United
1968 Manchester City
1967 Manchester United
1966 Liverpool
1965 Manchester United
1964 Liverpool
1963 Everton
1962 Ipswich Town
1961 Tottenham Hotspur
1960 Burnley
1959 Wolverhampton
  Wanderers
1958 Wolverhampton
  Wanderers
1957 Manchester United
1956 Manchester United
1955 Chelsea
1954 Wolverhampton
  Wanderers
1953 Arsenal
1952 Manchester United
1951 Tottenham Hotspur
1950 Portsmouth
1949 Portsmouth
1948 Arsenal
1947 Liverpool

Scotland

2003 Rangers
2002 Celtic
2001 Celtic
2000 Rangers
1999 Rangers
1998 Celtic
1997 Rangers
1996 Rangers
1995 Rangers
1994 Rangers
1993 Rangers
1992 Rangers
1991 Rangers
1990 Rangers
1989 Rangers
1988 Celtic
1987 Rangers
1986 Celtic
1985 Aberdeen
1984 Aberdeen
1983 Dundee United
1982 Celtic
1981 Celtic
1980 Aberdeen
1979 Celtic
1978 Rangers
1977 Celtic
1976 Rangers
1975 Rangers
1974 Celtic
1973 Celtic
1972 Celtic
1971 Celtic
1970 Celtic
1969 Celtic
1968 Celtic
1967 Celtic
1966 Celtic
1965 Kilmarnock
1964 Rangers
1963 Rangers
1962 Dundee
1961 Rangers
1960 Heart of Midlothian
1959 Rangers
1958 Heart of Midlothian
1957 Rangers
1956 Rangers
1955 Aberdeen
1954 Celtic
1953 Rangers
1952 Hibernian
1951 Hibernian
1950 Rangers
1949 Rangers
1948 Hibernian
1947 Rangers

FA CUP

Below are the post-war winners and runners-up of the FA Cup. An asterisk denotes that extra time was played. Some games went to replays – the first game's score is in brackets.

2003 Arsenal 1 Southampton 0
2002 Arsenal 2 Chelsea 0
2001 Liverpool 2 Arsenal 1
2000 Chelsea 1 Aston Villa 0
1999 Manchester United 2
  Newcastle United 0
1998 Arsenal 2 Newcastle
  United 0
1997 Chelsea 2
  Middlesbrough 0
1996 Manchester United 1
  Liverpool 0
1995 Everton 1 Manchester
  United 0
1994 Manchester United 4
  Chelsea 0
1993 Arsenal 2 Sheffield
  Wednesday 1 (replay
  after 1-1)
1992 Liverpool 2
  Sunderland 0
1991 Tottenham Hotspur 2
  Nottingham Forest 1*
1990 Manchester United 1
  Crystal Palace 0 (replay
  after 3-3)
1989 Liverpool 3 Everton 2*
1988 Wimbledon 1
  Liverpool 0
1987 Coventry City 3
  Tottenham Hotspur 2*
1986 Liverpool 3 Everton 1
1985 Manchester United 1
  Everton 0*
1984 Everton 2 Watford 0
1983 Manchester United 4
  Brighton and Hove
  Albion 0 (replay after
  2-2)
1982 Tottenham Hotspur 1
  QPR 0 (replay after
  1-1)
1981 Tottenham Hotspur 3
  Manchester City 2
  (replay after 1-1)
1980 West Ham United 1
  Arsenal 0
1979 Arsenal 3 Manchester
  United 2
1978 Ipswich Town 1
  Arsenal 0
1977 Manchester United 2
  Liverpool 1
1976 Southampton 1
  Manchester United 0
1975 West Ham United 2
  Fulham 0
1974 Liverpool 3 Newcastle
  United 0
1973 Sunderland 1 Leeds
  United 0
1972 Leeds United 1
  Arsenal 0
1971 Arsenal 2 Liverpool 1
1970 Chelsea 2 Leeds United
  1 (replay after 2-2)
1969 Manchester City 1
  Leicester City 0
1968 West Bromwich Albion
  1 Everton 0*
1967 Tottenham Hotspur 2
  Chelsea 1
1966 Everton 3 Sheffield
  Wednesday 2
1965 Liverpool 2 Leeds
  United 1*
1964 West Ham United 3
  Preston North End 2
1963 Manchester United 3
  Leicester City 1
1962 Tottenham Hotspur 3
  Burnley 1
1961 Tottenham Hotspur 2
  Leicester City 0
1960 Wolverhampton
  Wanderers 3 Blackburn
  Rovers 0
1959 Nottingham Forest 2
  Luton Town 1
1958 Bolton Wanderers 2
  Manchester United 0
1957 Aston Villa 2
  Manchester United 1
1956 Manchester City 3
  Birmingham City 1
1955 Newcastle United 3
  Manchester City 1

1954 West Bromwich Albion 3 Preston North End 2
1953 Blackpool 4 Bolton Wanderers 3
1952 Newcastle United 1 Arsenal 0
1951 Newcastle United 2 Blackpool 0
1950 Arsenal 2 Liverpool 0
1949 Wolverhampton Wanderers 3 Leicester City 1
1948 Manchester United 4 Blackpool 2
1947 Charlton Athletic 1 Burnley 0*
1946 Derby County 4 Charlton Athletic 1*

TOTAL FA CUP WINS
This list of winners includes all FA Cup competitions, from its beginnings in 1872.

10 – Manchester United

9 – Arsenal

8 – Tottenham Hotspur

7 – Aston Villa

6 – Blackburn Rovers, Liverpool, Newcastle United

5 – Everton, The Wanderers, West Bromwich Albion

4 – Bolton Wanderers, Manchester City, Sheffield United, Wolverhampton Wanderers

3 – Chelsea, Sheffield Wednesday, West Ham United

2 – Bury, Nottingham Forest, Old Etonians, Preston North End, Sunderland

1 – Barnsley, Blackburn Olympic, Blackpool, Bradford City, Burnley, Cardiff City, Charlton Athletic, Clapham Rovers, Coventry City, Derby County, Huddersfield Town, Ipswich Town, Leeds United, Notts County, Old Carthusians, Oxford University, Portsmouth, Royal Engineers, Southampton, Wimbledon

SCOTTISH CUP
Post-war winners of the Cup.

2003 Rangers
2002 Rangers
2001 Celtic
2000 Rangers
1999 Rangers
1998 Heart of Midlothian
1997 Kilmarnock
1996 Rangers
1995 Celtic
1994 Dundee United
1993 Rangers
1992 Rangers
1991 Motherwell
1990 Aberdeen
1989 Celtic
1988 Celtic
1987 St Mirren
1986 Aberdeen
1985 Celtic
1984 Aberdeen
1983 Aberdeen
1982 Aberdeen
1981 Rangers
1980 Celtic
1979 Rangers
1978 Rangers
1977 Celtic
1976 Rangers
1975 Celtic
1974 Celtic
1973 Rangers
1972 Celtic
1971 Celtic
1970 Aberdeen
1969 Celtic
1968 Dunfermline Athletic
1967 Celtic
1966 Rangers
1965 Celtic
1964 Rangers
1963 Rangers
1962 Rangers
1961 Dunfermline Athletic
1960 Rangers
1959 St Mirren
1958 Clyde
1957 Falkirk
1956 Heart of Midlothian
1955 Clyde
1954 Celtic
1953 Rangers
1952 Motherwell
1951 Celtic
1950 Rangers
1949 Rangers
1948 Rangers
1947 Aberdeen

EUROPEAN GLORY
For over four decades, teams from England and Scotland have enjoyed plenty of success on the continent. Below is a list of the British clubs that have made a final of a major European cup competition.

2003 Celtic, UEFA Cup, runners-up
2001 Liverpool, UEFA Cup, winners
2000 Arsenal, UEFA Cup, runners-up
1999 Manchester United, Champions League, winners
1995 Arsenal, Cup-Winners' Cup, runners-up
1994 Arsenal, Cup-Winners' Cup, winners
1991 Manchester United, Cup-Winners' Cup, winners
1987 Dundee United, UEFA Cup, runners-up
1985 Everton, Cup-Winners' Cup, winners
1985 Liverpool, European Cup, runners-up
1984 Liverpool, European Cup, winners
1984 Tottenham Hotspur, UEFA Cup, winners
1983 Aberdeen, Cup-Winners' Cup, winners
1982 Aston Villa, European Cup, winners
1981 Liverpool, European Cup, winners
1981 Ipswich Town, UEFA Cup, winners
1980 Nottingham Forest, European Cup, winners
1980 Arsenal, Cup-Winners' Cup, runners-up
1979 Nottingham Forest, European Cup, winners
1978 Liverpool, European Cup, winners
1977 Liverpool, European Cup, winners
1976 Liverpool, UEFA Cup, winners
1976 West Ham United, Cup-Winners' Cup, runners-up
1975 Leeds United, European Cup, runners-up
1974 Tottenham Hotspur, UEFA Cup, runners-up
1973 Liverpool, UEFA Cup, winners
1973 Leeds United, Cup-Winners' Cup, runners-up
1972 Tottenham Hotspur, UEFA Cup, winners
1972 Rangers, Cup-Winners' Cup, winners
1972 Wolverhampton Wanderers, UEFA Cup, runners-up
1971 Leeds United, UEFA Cup, winners
1971 Chelsea, Cup-Winners' Cup, winners
1970 Manchester City, Cup-Winners' Cup, winners
1970 Arsenal, Fairs Cup, winners
1970 Celtic, European Cup, runners-up
1969 Newcastle United, Fairs Cup, winners
1968 Manchester United, European Cup, winners
1968 Leeds United, Fairs Cup, winners
1967 Celtic, European Cup, winners
1967 Rangers, Cup-Winners' Cup, runners-up
1967 Leeds United, Fairs Cup, runners-up
1966 Liverpool, Cup-Winners' Cup, runners-up
1965 West Ham United Cup-Winners' Cup, winners
1963 Tottenham Hotspur, Cup-Winners' Cup, winners
1961 Rangers, Cup-Winners' Cup, runners-up
1961 Birmingham City, Fairs Cup, runners-up
1960 Birmingham City, Fairs Cup, runners-up

INCREDIBLE RECORDS

Most capped players –
England – Peter Shilton (125)
Scotland – Kenny Dalglish (102)
Wales – Neville Southall (92)
N. Ireland – Pat Jennings (119)
Republic of Ireland – Tony Cascarino (88)

Youngest international cap –
Northern Ireland – Norman Whiteside (17 years 41 days)
Republic of Ireland – Jimmy Holmes (17 years 200 days)
Wales – Ryan Green (17 years 226 days)
England – Wayne Rooney (17 years 111 days)
Scotland – Denis La (18 years 235 days)

Most consecutive seasons in English top division –
Arsenal (77), Everton (49), Liverpool (39), Coventry City (34)

Highest FA Cup score –
Preston North End 26 Hyde 0 (1887)

Highest Scottish Cup score –
Arbroath 36 Bon Accord 0 (1885)

Highest score in Premiership match – Manchester United 9 Ipswich Town 0 (1995)

Glossary

Advantage rule A rule that allows the referee to let play continue after a foul if it is to the advantage of the team that has been fouled against.

Anchor A midfielder positioned just in front of, and given the job of protecting, the defence. An anchor player can help allow other midfielders to push further forwards.

Assistant referees Formerly known as linesmen, these officials assist the referee with his decision-making during the game.

Bicycle kick An overhead volley, usually a shot on goal.

Blind side A position on the opposite side of a defender from the ball.

Box The penalty area.

Cap Recognition given to a player for each international appearance made for his country.

Caution Another word for a yellow card.

Chip A ball lofted into the air, either as a pass from a player to a team-mate or as a shot. Also known as a lob.

Clearance Kicking or heading the ball out of defence.

Counter attack A quick attack by a defending team after it regains possession of the ball.

Cross Sending the ball from the side of the pitch towards the opposition's penalty area.

Direct free kick A kick awarded to a team because of a major foul committed by an opponent. A goal may be scored directly from the kick.

Direct play A method of attacking using long passes from defence that tend to bypass the midfield and go straight to the forwards.

Dribbling Moving the ball under close control with short kicks or taps.

Drop ball A way of restarting play that involves the referee releasing the ball for a player from each team to compete over once it has touched the ground.

Feinting Using fake moves of the head, shoulders and legs to deceive an opponent and put him off-balance.

Formation The way a team lines up on the field in relation to where the defenders, midfielders and forwards are positioned.

Handball The illegal use of the hand or arm by a player.

Indirect free kick A kick awarded to a team because of a minor foul or offence committed by an opponent. A goal cannot be scored directly from the kick but must instead be played to a team-mate first.

Laws of the game The 17 main rules of football as established and updated by FIFA.

Lay-off A short pass made by a forward to a team-mate who is to the side of, or behind, him.

Libero Another term for a sweeper.

Marking Guarding a player to prevent him from advancing the ball towards the net, making an easy pass or receiving the ball from a team-mate.

Narrowing the angle A goalkeeping technique involving the keeper moving out towards the on-ball attacker to narrow the amount of goal at which the attacker can aim a shot.

Obstruction When a defensive player, instead of attempting to win the ball, uses his body to prevent an opponent from playing it.

Overlap To run outside and beyond a team-mate down the sides of the pitch in order to create space and a possible passing opportunity.

Professional foul A foul committed intentionally by a player, stopping an opposition attacker from a clear run on goal.

Set piece A planned play or move that a team uses when a game is restarted with a free kick, penalty kick, corner kick, goal kick, throw-in or kick-off.

Shielding A technique used by the player with the ball to protect it from a defender closely marking him. The player in possession keeps his body between the ball and the defender.

Square pass A simple pass made by a player to a team-mate running alongside him.

Stamina The ability to maintain physical effort over long periods. All players require good levels of stamina to stay effective over an entire match.

Stoppage time Time added to the end of any period to make up for time lost due to a major halt in play such as treating an injured player. Also known as injury time.

Sudden death A type of extra-time period during which the first goal scored by a team ends the game and gives that team the victory. The first goal is known as the 'golden goal'.

Sweeper A defender who can be played closest to his own goal behind the rest of the defenders, or in a more attacking role, and who is responsible for bringing the ball forwards.

Tactics Methods of play used in an attempt to outwit and beat an opposition team.

Target man A tall striker, usually the player furthest upfield, at whom team-mates aim their forward passes.

Through ball A pass to a team-mate that puts him beyond the opposition's defence and through on goal.

Volley Any ball kicked by a player when it is off the ground.

Wall A line of defenders standing close together to protect their goal against a free kick.

Wall pass A quick, short pair of passes between two players that sends the ball past a defender. Also known as a 'one-two'.

Weight The strength of a pass.

Zonal marking A system by which defenders mark opponents who enter their particular area of the pitch.

Websites

The Internet is full of thousands of websites devoted to particular teams, players or aspects of football, so it is a good idea to research your area of interest through a search engine. Below, we've detailed some of the most interesting and informative websites currently available.

www.360soccer.com
This site provides a strong international look at the global game, with sections on each continent's soccer news and reports. It is packed with links to sites focused on football in specific countries. This site is very interesting and well worth a visit.

www.footballreferee.org
The Internet home of the official referees' association. With tips on how to become an official, news, views and tests, this site is a must-visit for all budding referees.

www.clivegifford.co.uk
The author's website which, under the In-Print section, features regularly updated football tips and links to other webpages.

www.thecoachingcorner.com/soccer/index.html
A good, thorough grounding in the rules and tactics of the game.

www.the-fa.org
The Internet home of the Football Association, which runs the game in England.

www.fifa.com
FIFA's official site is huge and takes time to surf around. But stick with it as there's masses of data, helpful factsheets and the latest version of the laws of the game. There are also links to the governing bodies for football in each continent.

www.footballgroundguide.co.uk
This website gives directions, details and reviews of all 92 English and Welsh teams playing in the Football League or Premiership. Invaluable for travelling football fans.

http://web.onetel.net.uk/~carlholl/
Think you know your football? A visit to Carl's Football Quiz website will put you to the test. There are dozens of complete quizzes here and you can even send in your own questions.

www.precision-goalkeeping.com
Great website devoted to the art of goalkeeping; featuring legends, news and plenty of tips and techniques.

www.scottishfa.co.uk
The Internet home of the Scottish Football Association. The website includes details of the Scottish national team, player profiles and reports on previous international matches.

www.soccerbase.com
A terrific database of results, tables, players, transfers and other statistics on the game in Britain can be found at this website.

www.soccerhighway.com
Another great international football website with player votes and links to hundreds of other sites devoted to European, African, American and Asian football.

www.soccerlinks.co.uk/pages
Contains over 4,500 links to soccer websites devoted to particular clubs, leagues or topics in football. This site is particularly strong on links to youth and women's football sites.

www.uefa.com
A relaunched site for the authorities that govern European football, these pages feature lots of in-depth reports and analysis of UEFA Cup and Champions League matches and teams.

www.worldsoccer.com
The online version of World Soccer magazine, this site has news on all the major competitions, plus exclusive player profiles, interviews and features, as well as fixtures, results and tables.

www.worldstadiums.com
As its name suggests, this is a site devoted to the venues in which the game of football is played all over the world. It is a massive site searchable by country or stadium name.

Index

ACKNOWLEDGMENTS

Photographs in this book have been supplied by Empics, except the following:
Key: b = bottom, c = centre, l = left, r = right, t = top

4 bl Still Pictures; 5 tr Popperfoto, br Rex Features; 8 tl The National Football Museum, cr The National Football Museum, br Corbis, bl The National Football Museum; 9 t The National Football Museum, tl Robert Opie Collection, cl The National Football Museum, c The National Football Museum, cr The National Football Museum, bc The National Football Museum, br The National Football Museum; 10 bc www.umbro.com, bc www.umbro.com; 11 bl Allsport UK Ltd/Gary M.Prior, bc Colorsport; 17 c www.umbro.com, c The National Football Museum, cr The National Football Museum; 30 bl Colorsport; 33 tr Popperfoto; 35 c Wall 2 Wall Futbol, cr Wall 2 Wall Futbol; 51 br Allsport UK Ltd; 57 br Colorsport; 61 c Colorsport; 62 cr Colorsport, bl Hulton Getty; 63 tr Hulton Getty; 68 tl Hulton Getty; 69 tl Popperfoto/Ray Green, cr Popperfoto/Yves Herman; 70 cr Robert Opie Collection, cr Robert Opie Collection; 71 tl Popperfoto; 72 cl Hulton Getty, cr www.asromacalcio.it/sito-ufficiale/index.html, br pictures courtesy of Sky Sports; 73 c Colorsport, br Colorsport; 74 tl Popperfoto, cl Allsport UK Ltd; 75 tr Allsport UK Ltd/Jamie McDonald; 76 t Popperfoto, tl Colorsport, tr Popperfoto; 78 c Colorsport, cr Hulton Getty; 80 tl www.psg.fr, tr www.psg.fr.
The publishers would like to give special thanks to Jen Little at Empics.

Every effort has been made to trace the copyright holders of the photographs. The publishers apologize for any inconvenience caused.